S0-APN-269

new madrid

New Madrid: A Journal of Contemporary Literature
Volume II Number 2
Summer 2007

New Madrid is the official journal of the low-residency M.F.A. Program at Murray State University. It takes its name from the New Madrid seismic zone, which falls within the central Mississippi Valley and extends through western Kentucky. Between 1811 and 1812, four earthquakes with magnitudes greater than 7.0 struck this region, changing the course of the Mississippi River, creating Reelfoot Lake in Tennessee and ringing church bells as far away as Boston.

The editors invite submissions of poetry, fiction and creative non-fiction. All submissions must be via e-mail attachment, in MS-word format, to *newmadrid@murraystate.edu*, with a brief bio as the e-mail message. Submissions will be accepted only during two reading periods: Jan. 15 to Apr. 15 and Aug. 15 to Nov. 15. Check our website for specific guidelines and announcements of special issues.

Website: *www.newmadridjournal.org*

Copyright © 2007 by Murray State University

ISBN: 978-0-9791319-2-9

Subscriptions: $15.00 annually for two issues.

Please send subscription requests to:

The Editors, *New Madrid*
Department of English and Philosophy
Murray State University
7C Faculty Hall
Murray, KY 42071-3341

Front Cover: Sarah Gutwirth, *Kabinet 2006*, oil on canvas, 22 x 22",
Collection of Yvonne Bless.

Back Cover: Sarah Gutwirth, *Kabinet 2006* (detail)

new madrid

EDITOR
Ann Neelon

ADVISORY AND
CONTRIBUTING EDITORS
Squire Babcock
Brian Barker
Dale Ray Phillips

GRAPHIC DESIGN
Jim Bryant

ASSISTANT MANAGING EDITOR
Jack Cobb

M.F.A. EDITORIAL BOARD
Jeremy Byars
Tim Carter
Gregory Hagan
Glenn Jackson
Leif Erickson Rigney
Mark Spears
Jenna Wright

TABLE OF CONTENTS

Book Reviews

EDITOR'S INTRODUCTION
Ann Neelon

IN 1992, IN a case that came to be known as *Sheff vs. O'Neill,* lawyers for the ACLU, the NAACP and a number of other organizations together sued the state of Connecticut to bring attention to the egregiousness of the chasm in educational quality between school districts in inner-city Hartford and those in surrounding suburbs. Gladys Hernandez, an elementary school teacher in Hartford, gave testimony from her experience of taking students on an annual field trip to a zoo or farm. "The most extraordinary thing happened when they came to the river," she said. "They all stood up in a group and applauded and cheered, and I was aware they were giving the river a standing ovation. And they were so happy to see the beauty of the river, something that most of us go back and forth [across] and never take time to look at."

We'd like to see *New Madrid* speak to readers with as much depth and beauty as that river spoke to those children. We live in the middle of the country, in the area some on the East and West coasts are wont to dismiss as "the flyover zone." We believe that our pages can attest to the thousands of lives being lived fully and deliberately here. The Ohio, the Tennessee, The Mississippi and the Cumberland all flow through these parts and define us geographically and psychologically with their length and breadth. We are proud to publish a good number of writers from the Four Rivers Region in this issue. We are also proud to publish a good number of writers from outside. We recognize the danger of nostalgia about the homeplace, and we trust that over the years we will be able to establish a dynamic balance between home and away. As Simone Weil realized, "We must take the feeling of being at home into exile. We must be rooted in the absence of a place."

This issue marks the inauguration of the Wylder Center for the Literary Arts. The mission of the Wylder Center—which incorporates the MSU Reading Series, *Notations* (our undergraduate magazine), the Jesse Stuart Kentucky Writer Series, the Young Authors Camp, our low-residency M.F.A. program, *New Madrid*, etc.—is to celebrate writers and writing in the broadest context possible. We hope that like Deb Wylder, the prime mover of the Creative Writing program at Murray State, the Center will prove a singularly dynamic force both in the practice of the literary arts and in the dissemination of knowledge about them. In 1923, Murray State University was chartered as a Normal School with the training of teachers as its specific mandate. As a regional state university, Murray State has continued to define excellence first and foremost in terms of its service to teachers and teaching. Thus it is particularly fitting that the Wylder Center focus on outreach to the public schools as its goal for 2007-2008.

Our Book Review section—which offers our M.F.A. students the opportunity to test their mettle against more established writers—also celebrates its debut with this issue. Please consider sending recently released books of poetry, fiction and non-fiction to us for review in future issues.

We owe a special debt of thanks to Eric Gansworth for having served as talent scout for this issue. We sincerely appreciate all his work in the field, which generated an embarrassment of riches in terms of submissions. Furthermore, we hope to feature his own good work at a later date.

Here's hoping this issue offers you the sinuousness of a great river—lots of twists and turns and even a few epiphanies en route to the horizon.

Soldiers

Leah Stewart

Fort Bragg 1944

WHEN THE TRAIN from Richmond stopped, I was dreaming. The porter
stood over me saying, "Miss, miss, Fayetteville," and I opened my eyes and
tried to understand who he was and what he wanted me to do. In the dream
I'd gone to an enormous building, where all the surfaces were shiny, the
floors were enormous conveyer belts, and everywhere I went someone gave
me exactly what I wanted. I'd carried a cup that was repeatedly filled with
silver liquid, like mercury.

And now I was on a train, with a porter looking at me expectantly, so I
stood up and gathered my things and pretended to know what was happen-
ing, even though he and everything else kept on seeming like a dream. Certainly it seemed no part of reality to alight from a train at three in the morning, in a town I'd never seen, in a part of the country I'd never seen, with no
idea of how to reach my destination. I'd assumed some official person would
be at the station to meet me, but I'd been wrong. The streets were deserted
and dark. There was no sign of a taxi or a bus. I was supposed to get to Fort
Bragg. For the first time in my life I seemed to be entirely dependent on my
own resources, and I have to tell you that as I stood there on the platform
in a daze they seemed awfully limited. Among other lacks, I had no sense of
direction whatsoever, and no father to shout after me, "Where do you think
you're going?" as I wandered to the right while everyone else turned left. I
had a strong desire to cry. I began to imagine the look my father would give
me if I did cry, if I just sat down on my suitcase, put my face in my hands,
and gave up, waiting for something to magically transport me to the army.
I started walking. I was a 2nd lieutenant now, even if I didn't yet have the
uniform to prove it. I was twenty-three years old.

Across the street there was a building with a single dim light in the
window. I headed that way, half-carrying, half-dragging my bags. The sign
above the door read Fayetteville Hotel. As I pushed through the door into
the lobby, I tried to ignore the panicky feeling that I was going to the wrong
place, that I'd be inside while my imaginary official fruitlessly searched for
me outside. I told myself that at the very least I could get a room and find a
way to Fort Bragg in the morning. I was so focused on this that it took me
a moment to realize there were three other women in the lobby, about my
age, all with an air of dazed expectance, all strangers to me. They looked
at me like they knew me, because of course they instantly recognized me as
one of their own. I'd find out shortly that we were all assigned to the 54th
Field Hospital, and that whatever happened to us next would happen to us
together. Even before I knew that, I had the thought that soon these girls

might be my closest companions, a notion that seemed no more real than anything else that had happened so far.

"Hi girls," I said. "I'm Lucy Riley."

"Pleased to meet you," the first one said. "I'm Alice Howse." She'd been barefoot when I walked through the door, her feet tucked under her in the chair, but now she hastily slipped her shoes back on. She sat up straight and folded her hands in her lap, actually blushing a little, as though I'd caught her naked. Alice had a round, soft face, made-up just enough to be feminine, with powder and the red lipstick everybody wore. All this, and her sweet smile, suggested that she was kind and possibly pious, with a strong sense of the proprieties. She spoke with a southern accent, and although I had limited experience in this area I identified it as a genteel one. She asked, like a hostess, "Did you have a pleasant trip?"

I'd spent three days on various trains, starting in Passaic, New Jersey, and I was so tired and dislocated and hungry that bewilderment seemed to be my permanent state. "Well, I got here," I said. Then I added, because there was something about Alice that compelled me, "Thank you."

Alice said, "This is Madeline Hickey," and gestured at the girl to her right, who held herself like someone who knows she's pretty. She was blonde and buxom, with carefully arched eyebrows, blue eyes, high cheekbones, long legs, the Betty Grable of the nursing set. Madeline Hickey said, "Hello," and as she did she tilted her head slightly and patted at her hair, with a false, flirtatious shyness. I wanted to tell her that I was not a man, there was no need to do that act for me. She seemed the type who doesn't know how to behave with other women, who lights up with relief as soon as a man walks in the room. I suppose it's obvious I disliked her on sight, an animal response over which I had no control.

"Nice to meet you," I said, doing my best to sound like I meant it.

The third girl said, "I'm Marilyn Kay," and as I turned from Madeline to her she grinned at me as though she knew exactly what I'd been thinking. She had a Mediterranean complexion, dark, mischievous eyes. Her hair was a rich brown, almost black, and she wore it in a pixie cut—this at a time when everyone, myself included, wore their hair rolled back, pinned, and curled, with varying degrees of attractiveness. She was slumped down in her chair like she'd been sleeping, or pretending to, and her only concession to the niceties of introductions was to lift her head slightly from the back of the chair when I said my name. After Alice's careful posture and Madeline's coy preening, Marilyn Kay seemed like she just did not give a damn.

So that is what I thought of them at first. You can judge later whether those impressions were wrong. And what did they think of me? For the most part people are too polite to tell you what they think of you, and so it's hard to know. I'm a small person, barely five foot one, and back then I weighed just over a hundred pounds, so maybe they thought I wasn't very strong. I was wearing glasses, so maybe they thought I was bookish, and I gave them a closed-lip smile, because I was self-conscious about my slight overbite, so maybe they thought I was insecure about my looks. True enough, but they were wrong if they thought all this meant I was also sweet and shy. Sweet I have rarely been, and if on occasion I have kept my counsel I've never considered myself shy. I'm sarcastic, skeptical, critical. Here I'm only repeating what I've often been told. Apparently I'm known to possess a withering look: one raised eyebrow, narrowed eyes. I see nothing wrong with this look, or with sarcasm, both necessary tools to negotiating the world.

But I'm jumping ahead, quoting my children, and the people who've worked for me. Back in 1944 I might have been more cautious in my use of the withering look. Back then I was still the person who'd been told that she had little idea about life, having spent too much time locked up in the convent that was nursing school, too much time with her nose in a book. Most points of view are so limited. My father used to say that I was the smart one and my sister Clara was the pretty one, as if that was the end of the matter. In a way it was, because Clara dropped out of nursing school to get married and I stayed in. Maybe we should have known better than to take that assessment as both characterization and prophecy, but we were just children, after all.

"Where are you from, Lucy?" Alice asked, and I told her New Jersey. She said that she was from Murfreesboro, Tennessee, where she'd worked in a doctor's office, and Madeline was from Nashville, fresh out of nursing school at Vanderbilt.

I turned to Marilyn Kay, and asked, "Where are you from, Marilyn?" I sounded just like Alice.

"Houston," she said. "I've been working on a surgical ward, and I'm a little older than you babies—twenty-five. Oh, and I'm not Marilyn anymore. My name is too close to Madeline's so we've decided to call me Kay." In a stage whisper she added, "Madeline doesn't want to be known as Hickey." She grinned at me, and under the influence of that grin I said out loud, "Who can blame her?"

Kay laughed, Alice frowned, and Madeline pouted. She actually stuck out her lower lip like a child. She said, "Only men go by their last names."

"I must be a man, then," Kay said. She looked at her chest in mock alarm. "What do you suppose I'm doing with these?"

Now it was my turn to laugh. Poor Alice looked quite perturbed. "Well, Kay is a last name and a first name," she said, turning from Kay to Madeline as if hoping this information would create a truce between them.

"True enough," Kay said. I was still standing there like a spectator, and Kay pointed at an empty chair. "Have a seat," she said. "We're going to be here a while."

I did as she said and sat down. "What are we doing here?" I asked.

"We're waiting for the bus," Madeline said, as though the bus were coming to take us to prison. She sighed. "What have we gotten ourselves into?"

Alice patted Madeline's hand. I felt a flash of annoyance. "The army," I said. Madeline's expression said that she knew that, and didn't like it, and that furthermore she didn't like my tone.

Kay sang softly, "We're in the army now." She sunk down even lower in her chair and closed her eyes.

I thought I should probably do the same, and get some sleep while I had the chance, but the look on Madeline's face was goading me. I've never been good at keeping my mouth shut. "I don't know about you," I said, "but I'm glad to be here. I had to fight to get in. My eyesight's terrible, and the first doctor wanted to disqualify me. I had to talk him into letting me get a second opinion, and then I had to talk that doctor into signing a waiver."

Kay's eyes were open now, and she sat up, interested. "How'd you do it?"

"I asked him if he'd read about the nursing shortages. I told him keeping me out meant some of our boys wouldn't get the care they deserved. I said they needed me, and I had to go. I watched him sign that paper, and I was afraid until the last letter of his name he'd change his mind. Then I went and told my mother, because I'd thought there was no point in telling her until I knew I was going."

That had been a scene, telling my mother and Clara what I'd done, though not in the way I'd imagined. There was no yelling or crying. Clara took the news with a mournful, slightly bitter, calm, like someone she knew had just died without leaving her anything in the will. But my mother, my theatrical mother, who dressed for dinner and called me "cherie" and referred to her cramped living room as the "parlor," she didn't scold or fret or pace and wring her hands. She just turned ashen. She already had a husband and a son in the army. She hadn't expected to add a daughter. She looked at me like I was already a ghost.

"I did that, too," Kay said, pleased. "I mean, joined without telling my parents."

"Oh my," Alice said. "I would never have done such a thing." Her cheeks flushed at the very idea. She said, in a smaller voice, "Not that there wasn't some difficulty about it." I waited, expecting a story, but Alice looked away. "What do you think it will be like?" she asked. "Basic training, I mean."

"I don't know," Kay said. She laughed, like she'd just been struck by this realization. "I really don't."

"We'll do lots of hiking," I said. "I read an article, in the *American Journal of Nursing*. The girl who wrote it was very proud of how much hiking they'd done, because it wasn't easy. They hiked in army shoes. In the mud. And the shoes got caked in mud." I trailed off. This seemed a paltry bit of information, and I tried to retrieve some other detail from the article. As I was thinking, I realized Madeline was staring at me. She'd been so quiet the last few minutes, I'd thought her cowed, but she didn't look cowed at all. Her gaze was level, all that girlishness gone.

"Maybe I didn't have to make any patriotic speeches to get in," she said, "but I'm here, same as you. The difference between us is I'm not afraid to admit I'm scared."

"I'm not scared," I said.

"Of course you're not," Kay said. "Neither am I."

And then even Alice said, softly, "Neither am I."

"Is that right," Madeline said. "Well then I guess I'm not scared either."

We were so much younger than we realized. We sat there in the lobby of the Fayetteville Hotel, in the quiet hours before our lives changed in ways we couldn't yet imagine, and contemplated how utterly not scared we were. ◆

War in Spring
Don Boes

Instead of staring
at the war on TV
I should concentrate
on my own yard work:
gather some branches
knocked down
by last week's storm.
Straighten the brick border
around the curbside hawthorn.
Deal with the dandelions.
After the hourly bombing updates
I'll sweep the sidewalk
and clip the ivy
to within an inch of the ground.
Although I like to see
a dictator toppled
as much as the next guy,

my fence is leaning
and my gutters
are choked with leaves.
In my spare time,
I like to avoid conflict.
When a soldier dies,
the network flashes
a yearbook photo
of the fallen one.
When the weather
turns civil,
a woodpecker
returns to the yellowwood
outside my window.
The fewer chores
I do today, the fewer
I'll do tomorrow.

Bulldozers

Don Boes

Now they creep from site to acquired site,
yellow blades grimy with another leveled hollow,

treads gouging the shoulders of state roads
until at quitting time they park and steam

while their operators, bones rattled
by all that flattening, travel toward shelter,

the asphalt smooth beneath warming tires,
the evening scraped and pointless.

Losing Streak
Don Boes

This morning my neighbor
chain-sawed his sorry apple tree
all the way to the ground.
He's an assistant basketball coach,
newly fired by the university,
his tiny headshot

stuck at the bottom
of the newspaper column
documenting the latest loss.

Now he can admire
the lopsided water tower
on the next block and so can I.
Like Yogi Berra declared,
it's amazing what you can observe
just by watching. I was lucky,
after weeks of rummaging,
to locate Duchamp's nude
descending the staircase.

Her dainty cubist mouth
still escapes me. By no means
does she resemble Scarlett Johansson

so my disappointment is great.
Mushy apples plastered his driveway
regardless of the season.
No replacement has been named
and the losing streak continues.
A national search is likely.
All my information
comes from junk mail
and from citizens

I already know
and from open sky
and from sawdust.

Braveness in Three Sentences

Margrethe Ahlschwede

Sentence One

NOW THIS IS braveness, being asked to wait on the other side of the open doorway from where the airport security guard sits, he with a cell phone saying into it, "Gate," while at the same time saying to you, his eyes making strong eye contact, stay there, and then again being back on the walkie talkie saying, "Gate," and the Gate talking, making a bell sound, and he saying, "All right, you can come through now," and you saying, "A talking gate," and he responding with a chuckle and saying, "Go right over there, on the other side of the wall," and you do because you want to fly out of this airport and get home which you will not be able to do if you do not follow directions, if you begin to act, talk, or look in any way like you might be a terrorist, which you do not, since you are a grandmother and a writer and a teacher, but none of these people know that because they are hired to know the rules and enforce the rules which since January have said that people such as you who use wheelchairs and wear braces—and prostheses, you learned at the Nashville airport where this airplane ride started—must have more security checks because security personnel have found knives and last week a gun on a person such as yourself—but not such as yourself because you are not carrying a gun and you are not carrying a knife—and so must have more inspection than your husband who is walking through the metal detector having taken off his belt with the metal buckle and put it on the conveyer belt along with his backpack, your book bag, and his metal watch, but this time having to take off his shoes because Rockports, he reports later according to the TSA employee, have metal shanks and he's wearing his bowling shoes by Rockport and you see him watching you as you roll by the conveyer belt over to a place signaled by the TSA employee who asks you to wait, who calls over to her female co-worker, "female body check," and to which the co-worker responds, "let me get my gloves on" and as she says this she struggles (you imagine she's struggling because of her running narrative but you are not looking, not in the least being attentive to what she is doing with her hands because you already know what will be ahead and the words "invasive," "intrusive" run through your mind as does the thought that if Senator Bill Frist's wife or Senator Lamar Alexander's wife had to undergo this kind of searching neither Senator Frist nor Senator Alexander would stand for it, not for a minute, this searching that is about to start, and it does), the security employee now having pulled on her blue gloves and her narration continues and you listen wanting to be out of there, wanting not to have to be screened this way, wanting to say, but I'm not a terrorist, I'm a grandmother, a writer and a

teacher, but knowing were you to scream this you would be escorted somewhere else and it could take hours or days—your imagination stops after
this—for you to be allowed to fly because of the fuss you made and because
you are suspicious-looking still and you hear the narration from the woman
who is about your height and wears a white shirt with a pocket, a name tag
on a lavaliere, black pants and belt, her hair colored a dark rosy-brown, at
least that's the way it looks as she bends forward in front of you, "now I'm
going to put my hands like this" as she demonstrates what could be the
arm motions to identify the Cross-Your-Heart Bra, "my hands of course
will be turned out," she demonstrates and begins to swipe the backs of her
hands between your breasts top to bottom and underneath "and now I will
check under your arms, my hands of course like this" she says again as she
demonstrates by holding her hands so the backs would smash if she crashed
her hands together, "and would you lean forward, and I will be using the
backs of my hands" and she does that again the backs of her hands up and
down "and now I will put my hands under your buttocks" and she does "to
feel if there's anything in your cushion" and you could tell her nothing but
air, but that would not matter since she has a job to do "and would you put
your arms out" and you do remembering having heard a woman from your
department returning from an air flight describing the scarecrow pose and
showing the scarecrow pose right there in the front office, and now the
screener says, "I need to swipe your braces and your shoes and we can do
that over here" as she points to a room around to your right where the door
doesn't immediately open and she says "I wonder if Jack remembered to
unlock the door" and another security person, this one male—is it Jack or
not-Jack—walks toward the locked door, pulls out a key, unlocks the door,
and my security person opens the door and motions for me to follow her
into this room which seems like a small storage closet with a light for the
small table that's there, two chairs (she hauls one of them out of the way
and onto the table top), a cabinet, the first security person following and
she closes the door after which the other security person given to narrating
pulls my pants leg up to my knee and swipes one Velcro strap, one side of
the plastic upright around the back of my calf, and pulls my pant leg down
and says as she swipes the back of my shoe, "and here where you put your
shoe on" and then my shoe, each leg, all the while counting and now she's
up to eight and says "I only can do eight" and hands the plastic wand with
the small square of cloth to the other security helper and says "this will
only take a minute or two" as we wait until the first security person comes
back with the wand with the cloth in the end and says "this is all clear,"
and the narrator security person takes two more swipes, one swipe over the

blue batting glove I'm wearing on my left hand, another swipe over the blue batting glove I'm wearing on my right hand and we wait again until the first security person comes back and she says "all clear" and I ask "and you don't have to check the top Velcro bands on my thighs?" and she looks at me and says she has patted that with her hand and she is not suspicious and I say good and I leave knowing I have not said much, knowing I have felt so alienated from who I believe I am and what I believe I do and that I can't wait to get out of there, can't wait to get home, can't wait to be done with flying for this violation of who I am, the suspicions that have been raised around someone like me who uses a wheelchair but, I say again with emphasis, not like me, because I am a writer and a teacher and a reader and a grandmother and a quiltmaker and I was born in Denmark and I grew up in Nebraska and when I was sixteen I chose this country because I stood before a judge and swore I would be faithful to this country and I have a number and a U.S.A. official paper in a brown sleeve of an envelope that is filed at home under "important papers" and that I may have to take with me if I decide to travel to Canada and have to prove that yes, I am a citizen, I am not a terrorist, I am gainfully employed in real work, necessary work, and, again, I am not a terrorist, and I call on a lot of braveness to follow orders, to not raise suspicions, to act and look like I am not a terrorist because right now, on the surface of things, that is how I am identified, a potential terrorist.

Sentence Two

At the Nashville airport
on the way to San Antonio
security procedures
for people like me who use wheelchairs
and for people who wear prostheses
have heightened

and I now must
undress

but that's an exaggeration
because all I do is
slip my pants down
far enough
for the inspection wand
to wipe the Velcro on my upper leg band
plus I go through what has been common for years—
the hand patting all over, upper and lower body—
which hadn't seemed like such a violation

but undressing
even barely

is, even though the undressing
is in a separate room
(the security person raises a garage door
to a parking area for a small service vehicle)
with two security people present—
one to do the swiping with the wand,
the other to record who is in the room—
each of us—them, me, Bill—
and what transpired, Bill saying later
"That's to protect them," me feeling

violated

invaded

alien

Margrethe Ahlschwede

but hardly talking
and then only calmly
for fear
that any
resistance
would make me
to them
what the rules suspect
I am
a terrorist
with a gun
with a knife.

Sentence Three

    Along the San Antonio Riverwalk long boxy rafts with guard rails float
over the dark river water, a raft captain tour guide in a straw hat, golf shirt
and khakis narrates the experience, his narration amplified because of the
microphone he wears which looks just like the microphones pop stars wear
when they sing on stage, but this is not a stage, this is the San Antonio
Riverwalk and the passengers in the boxy boats hum over the water thread-
ing past terraces of shops and bars and restaurants with small white garden
tables and small white matching chairs arranged a hair behind the sidewalk
that has no guard rail, not even a tiny lip along the side nearest the river to
prevent an errant baby stroller, an errant wheelchair, and an errant walker
from spilling into the river and I think about terrorists, how there is no security guard here, no "please wait" and no gloved hands touching my body
and if there were, police would storm over, handcuffing the caresser, asking
me about the violation, the caresser being the terrorist, not I, even though
not one thing has changed except location where here on the Riverwalk
vendors carry back packs and shopping bags of blinking plastic wands and
mouths and lips and flowers that wink and nod in neon pink and green and
turquoise, where kids like miniature Darth Vaders walk against the flow
of pedestrians spritzing their magic wands on and off, showers of plastic
fireworks spitting out of the ends of their plastic wands, b-b gun-size pellets
nodding and blinking fluorescent dots from the plastic mouths and lips they
wear as costume, where at those small white tables margarita glasses with
wide deep bowls are half-full, now quarter-full, where melting beer-filled

glasses produce grey circles on the small paper napkin squares underneath them, where a woman with short straight silver hair pumps her leg up and down as she sits on the piano bench thumping her accompaniment for the trumpeter playing a trumpet with a longer, wider bell than a high school trumpet would have and who plays "Mood Indigo," and more hum-able tunes that fade as you meander the Riverwalk gaining ground on another kid coming toward you with a plastic fireworks-shooting wand, a mom and dad and a baby in a stroller, a grandma and a grandpa, her arm in his, dodging wide-eyed around oncoming girls in shorts and slight T-shirts and plastic sandals and bags that swing from their shoulders and boys in jeans that hang low or shorts with belts, another tune—this time a flute and a guitar—nearing, growing sweeter from under the umbrellas of the next outdoor bar and you think again about braveness and the airport where we all are under suspicion, and how here, only short blocks from the Alamo, in a braveness of trusting and trust, none of us is under suspicion, none of us, tonight. ■

Balloons & Boys

Peter Conners

I understand the impulse to celebrate bits of the boy in the balloons but the balloons are not the boy and the boy is not bits in the balloons. *Some are whispering. Hands are touching.* One day before I heard about the balloons traveling one hundred miles to land on the 14th hole of a golf course I spotted a skinny scared doe scampering down a dense city street with blood in its mouth. *We have not yet arrived at the section of disbelief.*

The man was a junkie with a necktie for his day in court. *Were there balloons mystifying overhead?* He pleaded for the police officers to believe his story: a skinny scared doe had just scampered down a dense city street with blood in its mouth. *Some are whispering. Elbows are nudging.*

There was an opportunity here for a bystander to free the man of his doubt and paranoia. The police officers were getting to him. *Have I moved this body before?* There was an opportunity for a bystander to combine the idea of bits of boy being projected into balloons mystifying one hundred miles into a city where a scared skinny doe scampered through midday traffic. There was an opportunity for us all to stand in doubt.

Old Growth Forest
Dixon Boyles

JEWEL HINTON WAITED until the death of Elford Sims before visiting Pine Haven Rest Home. Though the two men had become friends, it was with reluctance that Elford had entrusted Jewel with a letter addressed to Fern Ransdell along with the assurance that she had once been a beauty who had been the love of his life. He had gone on to say that she was now just an old woman who had reduced a lifetime of worry to the single desire not to be a burden to anyone. She might as well have wished for wings, Jewel thought, as he made his way through the gridlock of wheel chairs just inside the entrance. Eyes beseeched him from sagging faces which tilted and craned themselves toward him in such absent recognition and greed that it seemed that he might happily be devoured for his youth. He was forty.

Careful to remain just out of reach, Jewel approached the front desk where he was directed to the room of the venerable widow. He made his way down one of the several halls which extended from the reception area like the spokes of a wheel until he came to a door that was pushed to but not closed. He knocked several times, quietly and then louder, before nudging his way in.

Fern Ransdell sat across the room in a wide ramp of sunlight. Her back was to him, arms hanging loosely at her sides as if she were awaiting the rapture or dead, conjectures that were disproved by the snores which escaped her open mouth. On the dresser stood the photographs of family members arranged in no apparent hierarchy around the telephone. An impressive afghan, a vibrant black and orange, stretched across the bed, and Jewel would have left the letter there were its purpose not to facilitate an introduction to the old lady who owned some property which Jewel wished to purchase.

"Mrs. Ransdell," he began, gently shaking her shoulder for a moment before her eyes blinked open.

"You'll untie me, won't you, hon?" Her words were slurred and thick and he thought he must have misunderstood her until she repeated, "Won't you?"

He glanced down to see a strap stretched across her lap much like those used to secure luggage to the roof of a car. "I've got a letter for you, Mrs. Ransdell," he said. "It's from Elford Sims."

~~~

"But you'll untie me, won't you, hon?"

The name had no effect on her, and for a moment Jewel wondered if his friend had wooed her under the guise of an alias before deciding she was just senile. He wondered if she still possessed power of attorney. Buying the Ransdell tract could be greatly complicated if he had to deal with a group of heirs. Of course, he had no intention of freeing her, figuring that whoever had tied her there must have had a good reason, though for the life of him he couldn't see where she might run. Out the window, a large field of soybeans bordered the grounds of Pine Haven which apparently took its name from a spindly row of slash pine newly planted along its perimeter.

"Of course he won't untie you, Granny Fern," said a woman's voice from behind him. "You just sit there and enjoy your sunshine." Then to him, "You don't work here." It was a statement not a question.

By now he was facing her. "No ma'am, I don't," he managed to say, flustered at the awkwardness of the situation. At first glance, the woman was strikingly pretty despite heavy makeup, with long dark hair which hung to the shoulders of her blouse which, in turn, stretched immaculate and white into her jeans. As she reached Jewel however, her gray eyes fixed on him with a fixedness he would have expected from a figure in a wax museum. He wondered if she might be crazy.

"Well." Her smile was unsettling as well. Why would a complete stranger give him such a smile?

"I've got a letter for your grandmother." He paused. "She is your grandmother?" He guessed she was around thirty, and the scent of her perfume stirred in him a sense of opportunity.

"But you're not the mailman either."

He began to explain that Elford Sims had sent him when she interrupted, saying, "Why don't you just give it to me? I'll read it to her."

He wondered how he could explain that he was actually interested in the property without sounding like some used car salesman. "He told me to wait for an answer."

She stared at him and he stared back while his heart pounded and he hoped Granny Fern didn't suddenly regain her memory. "Who is this Elford Sims?" she said finally.

Jewel explained that Elford was an elderly friend of his but that he was uncertain of Elford's connection to Mrs. Ransdell. (After all, Jewel reasoned, people can be defensive about the human failings of ancestors.) "He would have delivered it himself, but he doesn't get out much these days." It wasn't exactly a lie.

"Well," she said, drawing out the word. "I'm afraid my grandmother's not been much for letter writing since her stroke." She nodded in the direction of Granny Fern who had nodded off herself.

Jewel's heart sank. He wondered how he might tactfully ask whether she still retained power of attorney. He decided that he had better focus on winning over the granddaughter. "Old Elford's pretty patient. But it did seem to mean a lot to him. Hell, you could probably make up an answer for him and he'd be happy. Just a note or something."

"You mean pretend I'm my grandmother." She seemed doubtful though her smile had returned.

"Oh no, nothing like that," he said, "just some sort of acknowledgement. Like I said it seemed important to him but I don't think he has any real expectations. I tell you what. Why don't I give you my number?—Elford never answers his phone—and if after you've read the letter to your grandmother she wants to contact him, I'll let him know."

"Mr. Hinton," she said, examining the business card he had handed her, "do you think he and my grandmother had some sort of affair." Her voice dropped to a whisper, and he leaned forward to catch her words.

"With all due respect," he said, "I know they did."

~~~

Jewel believed that Pamela would call for it was his business to know when someone wished to buy or sell, and he understood that few commodities are more enticing than romantic intrigue, particularly when it involves a family member. He was telling himself all this as he removed his snake guards from under the toolbox in the bed of his truck and laced them over his boots.

He wondered what Pamela had thought of the letter and was worried that it might begin with, "Dear Fern, By the time you read this I'll be dead, etc." a fact that Fern might already know. Despite her presumed senility, Jewel suspected she had her lucid moments. He could only hope that they would be indistinguishable from her normal confusion, at least until he had a chance to explain his lie.

He climbed over the gate which blocked the entrance to the Ransdell tract. Slashes of purple paint sprayed sporadically across random trees indicated the land was posted, but Jewel doubted he would see anyone. Hunting season had ended months ago, and Jewel observed that that the ruts traversing a nearby mudhole had not seen a tire in quite some time.

The road itself ran parallel to a good-sized creek. Jewel hoped no beavers had colonized the area. He remembered a cruise he and Elford had made in which they had discovered what had been projected to be a valuable tract had become a worthless bog of dead and dying hardwoods.

Elford often spoke of dynamiting beaver dams to prevent such flood-
ing in his own hardwood bottoms. They had stood under a limbless beech
along a creekbank in Hempstead County, surveying the beaver damage
when Elford had surprised Jewel by asking him why he wasn't married.

"I don't know ," Jewel had replied, face flushing. "I guess I don't have
time for love and all that shit."

"What else is there?" Elford had wanted to know. That is when Elford
first told him of Fern Ransdell. They had been sweethearts before Elford's
entry into World War II. Then while Elford was fighting the Japanese, Fern
had met and married Earl Ransdell who had finagled a deferment due to
his involvement in the oil industry which was deemed vital at that time.
According to Elford, Earl had been better at satisfying his government than
satisfying his wife for upon Elford's return, "We went at it like there was no
tomorrow. "

"Then why aren't you still together?"

The look that crossed Elford's face made Jewel wish he hadn't asked the
question. "Her children," the old man sighed, "that and the fact that some
things just aren't meant to be."

The angle of the sunlight overhead told Jewel that only a couple of hours
of good light remained. As he neared what appeared to be the end of the
road, he could see that a small clearing had been cut into the woods, and
upon closer approach the shape of a cabin began to emerge through the
picketed shadows of the trees. As he came closer, he spied a small well
house at the far end of the porch. Peering through a window Jewel saw
a large room with a rocking chair in front of a fireplace at one end and a
kitchen at the other. Through an open door he could make out the corner
of a bed. There was another closed door which Jewel decided must be a
bathroom. The presence of electrical outlets and overhead lights suggested
that the house was wired for electricity which he figured was supplied by
generator.

From the pocket of his brush jacket, he removed a section of map and
spread it across the roof of the well housing. The Ransdell property con-
tained nearly three hundred acres, far too large to cruise before dark. As he
calculated the shape of the property, Jewel imagined an overlay of intersect-
ing tangents in the form of a grid. Using a compass to maintain his first
such tangent, Jewel made his way across the creek and into the trees. At
twenty-five paces, he stopped and counted every tree of commercial value,
estimating its height and width, within the first "plot" of his imaginary
grid. In a thorough cruise, he would estimate each plot. Due to the failing
light, today he would only take every other plot. Even so, following the

configuration of his grid would ensure that he walked the entire property, thus observing any anomalies in the land which might present problems to a logging crew, such as the creek.

He determined fairly quickly that the tract was a valuable property. By contemporary standards, much of the forest was old growth which meant it had been logged before but not in several decades. The majority of the acreage lay along a ridge covered predominantly in pine. He noted the thin "pecan-shell" bark covered trees sixty feet or more with little taper. The thinness of the bark suggested slow growth and heart pine which supposedly no longer existed. Twenty or thirty years before, when loads were scaled not by the ton but by the log, with the board feet of each log estimated and priced accordingly, the Ransdell tract would have been even more valuable. Now, it would bring no more than the shaggy barked, coarse grained logs of slash pine cultivated in the plantations favored by the large corporations.

Still, Jewel could imagine managing such a forest into his old age. If he succeeded in buying the land, he would begin logging immediately. By select harvesting, he could recoup nearly half what he planned to offer just in saw logs to be milled into lumber. The pulpwood he would "leave standing. It would not only hold its present value but also generate even more wealth as it matured into saw logs in the years to come, a process that would be enhanced by the removal of the largest trees now. A good stand of hardwood was interspersed throughout as well: mostly white oak and hickory with a smattering of poplar, gum, and maple. Patches of white freckled the landscape, announcing the dogwoods which were now in bloom.

As he continued to work his grid, Jewel began to envision an even grander scheme. Situated on the outskirts of Texarkana, the property would make a splendid development. The creek could be dammed to create lakefront lots and perhaps he would set aside land for nature trails to attract the doctors and lawyers he imagined as his new neighbors. He would build a grand house himself and live there while he sold off parcels in the years to come. All his life, it seemed, had directed him to this moment where preparation had finally met opportunity. Such a property had the power to transform his life. He would find himself a good-looking woman, get married, and start a family. He thought of Pamela who might even stand to inherit the property soon.

Jewel hadn't set out to be alone. He had grown up believing that sooner or later everyone found the "right" person. At the age of forty, he was no longer certain. The good luck he had seen in his parents' marriage seemed to be the exception, and even they had begun to bicker in recent years. He had reached the point where he told people that he would "wait long as I can, then marry one young as I can," a joke that had never been funny and was even less so now.

His final tangent took him behind the cabin into an area dominated by the creek. He was no longer plotting trees, having already decided on the offer he would make. Cresting the ridge, he paused to enjoy the last of the sun. He removed his cap and wiped his brow before plunging into the briar thicket which separated him from what sounded like a waterfall at the base of the hill.

Once there, he discovered that his ears had not deceived him. At the end of a long riffle, the stream seemed to disappear into the shadow of a massive cottonwood, and closer inspection revealed that having cut as far as it could into a shelf of limestone, the water had here found more yielding soils creating a small waterfall. Some creature slid off a partially submerged log into a surprisingly deep pool at the base of the falling water. By now, Jewel was thirsty and regarded the clear stream with regret. He could recall having drunk from several such streams in his youth before the byproducts of modern chicken farms had rendered all such behavior reckless. Why not dam the stream, Jewel rationalized, it was ruined already.

~~~

At home he replayed his messages. The first two were business, but the third presented a problem that would challenge a psychic. Pamela had called to say that she had a letter for Elford Sims but that she thought it would be nice if they could set up a reunion between Elford and her grandmother. "Not without Dr. Kevorkian," Jewel thought as he listened to the message three more times in an attempt to decipher what he could hear in her voice. He asked himself if he had rather have Pamela or the property and decided to go for a package deal. Looking out the window at two squirrels chasing each other around the trunk of a white oak, he dialed her number.

He stared into the approaching night and wondered what Elford would do. "Elford's gone shy on me," he heard himself saying when she picked up the phone. He went on to say that maybe it would be better if Jewel could read him the letter before they arranged a meeting. His heart thumped inside his chest like a piston threatening to break out of its crankcase. Why not just tell her the truth?

"If you really think so, but I have to warn you. Granny Fern really has her hopes up."

Jewel said he thought Elford did, too.

~ ~ ~

The next afternoon Jewel found himself seated across the kitchen table from Pamela, sipping iced tea while hummingbirds buzzed an apple-shaped feeder outside. They had been talking just long enough for Jewel's initial anxiety to turn into a good sort of nervousness, the kind that comes with knowing that you might close a deal. Pamela was saying after all these years it was exciting to find out that the great love of her grandmother's life wasn't even her grandfather.

"I don't know if I'd say that."

She said that was because Jewel had never met the man. It seems he had prayed about everything, especially vanity. Once Pamela had bragged about being the prettiest girl in her class and the old man had prayed with her for over an hour. She asked if Elford had ever mentioned him.

"Only to say he was one of those types who doesn't believe in luck even though they are born with a horseshoe in each pocket." On the wall behind her was a needlepoint that read "To Forgive Is Human, To Err is Divine."

"I don't know how she stayed with him all those years." She laughed. "I guess I do now. I tell you, when I read that letter, whew." She fanned her face with her hand. "I can't wait to meet him."

Jewel decided that now was as good a time as any. "I've got a confession to make. Elford's dead."

She gasped at the news. "This morning?"

Jewel admitted that Elford had been dead over a month. He explained that he had been trying to break the news to Granny Fern when she had walked into the room. "And when I saw you, I don't know, something came over me. I knew I wanted to see you again but wasn't sure the best way to go about it."

"So you figured lying to my grandmother was the best way." The gray eyes fixed upon him, but strangely she did not seem upset.

Jewel said he figured most old people read the obituaries anyway and that she probably knew. "Besides, no offense, but she wasn't exactly responsive."

Pamela inhaled deeply and released the breath abruptly. "All this just to ask me out."

Jewel shrugged apologetically.

"I'd love to, honey, but you should know that technically I'm married."

"What do you mean married?" He wondered if he was hearing things. A moment before he had flinched in anticipation of a broadside, and now he was having difficulty focusing on what Pamela was saying. His mind was racing. Even if romance was out, she could still act as a go-between on the land.

"What you call estranged, actually. Floyd thinks we'll get back together when he gets back from Iraq but…" she made a face and shuddered as if tasting something bitter.

A long pause ensued before he finally managed to bluster that he should have known that a good-looking woman like her would be already be taken and that he hadn't meant any offense in asking.

'Why should that offend me? Didn't I just say that I would love to go out?"

"But you're married," Jewel heard himself saying as if this fact was a surprise to her. He wondered again about her sanity. "And to a soldier."

"I said technically. And so was my grandmother, honey," she said, reaching across the table to squeeze his hand. "That didn't stop your friend Elford."

Jewel said he didn't know, that he would have to think about that. He doubted Pamela had done the needlepoint. Somehow it did not seem right to step out with the wife of a soldier in the war against terror. On the other hand, a deal this big (and a woman like Pamela) negated a lot of patriotism.

"Well, don't think too long. That's Floyd's problem."

"You're not mad about Elford?"

"I already knew truth be known. You were right about Granny reading the obituaries, said they used to be an item. I was just curious to see what you were up to." She squeezed his hand harder and told him she admired a man who would lie for love.

Jewel admitted that he had always been a romantic at heart. He calculated her demeanor before adding, "But since we are laying our cards on the table, I've got to tell you I'm also interested in your grandmother's property at the edge of town."

"You must mean the farm, but it's not for sale. At least while Granny is still alive. Says there are too many memories." Pamela went on to say that it really wasn't so much a farm as a bunch of woods with a hunting cabin. She had picnicked there often when she was a child. "Say," she wondered out loud, "you don't suppose that's where she and Elford…"

"He did seem to know a good deal about the lay of the land."

"I bet he did."

Jewel felt the heat come to his cheeks as he explained that wasn't what he meant. Was this how Fern had been with Elford? He had imagined silk rustling and breathless sighs, stolen moments in a shady grove, a tear stained pillow in a motor court. Maybe what had actually transpired was the sweaty collision of whisky-fueled bodies in the backseat of some sedan parked in a honky-tonk parking lot. The cars had been bigger then. Across the table, Pamela lifted her hair from her neck and pressed it against the back of her head. A few stray tendrils trailed downward like the remnants of some plant that has escaped its container, directing Jewel's gaze toward the trace of razor stubble beneath her arm exposed at the border of her pale blue t-shirt. He tried not to imagine her scent. He wasn't yet ready for what he thought would happen next. "Does she have power of attorney?" he asked.

Pamela dropped her hair and exhaled abruptly. She said nothing got by her grandmother, stroke or no stroke. It seems Jewel had simply caught her at a bad time. Maybe he would like to go on a picnic with them tomorrow.

~~~

A light but steady rain was falling as Jewel parked his truck. The puddles that hugged the parking lot dimpled briefly with each drop in the manner of small fish gasping for air. He was deliberately early, hoping to catch Mrs. Ransdell while she was still sharp. He also hoped to speak with her privately.

He could hear the bray of her television from the hall. Someone was explaining the "nuances" of polenta. He pushed the door open calling out a loud hello as he did. "What you watching there, Mrs. Ransdell?" he said as made his way toward her chair. "Looks like grits." Despite his air of nonchalance, he was uneasy about his plans.

She fumbled with her remote, and Jewel reached out and hit the power.

He introduced himself again and mentioned that he might be a little early for the picnic. He wondered if she could hear the muted thunder outside. She raised a hand, motley with age, to her hair and Jewel realized her hair had been done. "Why look at you?" he said. "Don't you have the prettiest hair?"

She accepted the compliment without acknowledgment. "Untie me, hon."

What could be the harm? He worked to free the strap from a buckle beneath the seat of the chair, surprised at the heat from her thighs. He had not expected such a confirmation of life. He told her that Elford had directed him to her. "Naturally, I wanted to meet you—he spoke so highly of you. Now, I see why."

"Never thought much of a liar." She formed the words carefully as if estimating the weight of each one before it escaped her mouth. Her lipstick, a gaudy red, stretched past the corners of her mouth, a fact he noticed in trying to avoid her stare.

He pondered what to say. Was she talking about him or Elford? "He also said you had some land I should try to buy before you died."

A frown furrowed her brow before she wheezed out what passed for a laugh. "That's more like it." She laughed again and Jewel searched somewhere in the sound for a trace of what must have drawn Elford years before but couldn't find it. She manipulated her lips in an effort to form the words which apparently trailed her thoughts. "How much do you think it's worth?"

Past experience had taught him that the question was a tricky one. He estimated the timber alone to be worth $3,000 an acre, not counting the land. But say she had the land figured at $2,000. If his initial offer was over that, he might spook her into seeking other bids. "I haven't seen it of course," he lied, "but land around here generally goes somewhere around $1500 an acre."

The long pause which followed told Jewel that she was impressed by the number. He felt an elation to realize that she was considering the offer. "What makes you think I want to sell?" she finally managed to say in a manner that might have passed as coquettish in someone other than a crone.

Jewel said that the obvious answer would be for the money but that he had a feeling that the place meant more to her than just money. He said that the land would eventually go to her heirs, he expected, and that while he had no doubts that they were all fine people they might not all agree on what to do with the property. The land could end up being parceled off, clear cut, and divided into trailer parks. There was nothing wrong with that, of course, but there weren't many properties like hers left. "In fact, I realize I may be tipping my hand, but when Elford described your place to me I knew I had to try to buy it."

The old lady whispered, "Is that all?" Her eyes were full and a flush had risen to her cheeks.

Jewel hesitated. He had only hoped to gain the old lady's good graces and he now sensed that the whole deal, his entire future, might hinge on what he said next. Taking a deep breath, he began to say something about Elford Sims when Pamela entered the room, announcing herself with a loud "Knock, knock" followed closely by "He's not trying to pull a fast one is he?"

She had apparently bathed in perfume, and as she unbuttoned her raincoat he could see that her peach blouse was unbuttoned to a level impossible to misinterpret. Swinging a picnic basket in her hand, she appeared ready for any appetite. What would her grandmother think? He heard something like a cough behind him and turned to Mrs. Ransdell who was shifting her jaw in an attempt to adjust her lower plate. Following a pair of rictus-inducing manipulations, she said that at her age even a fast one took a good while. Both the women cackled at that one.

The lights flickered in the simultaneous flash and crack of a lightning strike nearby. Despite himself, Jewel flinched though neither woman reacted in the slightest as if both had been born into such an element. "Maybe we ought to skip the picnic," he said. Mrs. Ransdell had his offer if she wished to sell.

Pamela said they weren't about to give up their picnic date with a good-looking man just because of a little rain. She promised they wouldn't melt.

~~~

They went in Jewel's truck with Granny Fern sitting up front while she went on about how good it was to get out of the house. Pamela sat behind her with her back braced against the rear door and her legs resting on the seat before her. Once when Jewel attempted to check for traffic when changing lanes, he found himself instead staring down the open throat of her blouse. Pamela cleared her throat, and he blushed as his eyes met hers. "Just checking my blind spot," he blustered.

"That was a twenty-twenty look if I ever saw one." She leaned toward him and pinched his cheek. "Just watch the road, honey. I'll let you know if anything gets in your way."

"You hear from Floyd?" Granny Fern twisted in the seat to face her granddaughter. She had refused to wear her seatbelt.

Pamela said she reckoned he was still making the world safe for democracy.

The old woman barked out a laugh then asked Jewel what he would call a man who would leave a woman like her granddaughter at home alone.

"A soldier?"

Both the women hooted with laughter. "A fool's what I told him," Pamela said. "I told him I was planning on sleeping with somebody and if he wanted it to be him he had better stick around."

Jewel couldn't help wondering if Fern had told Elford the same thing. They had reached the turnoff, and Jewel got out to unlock the gate with a key Pamela gave him. A few minutes later, Jewel held Granny Fern's arm as Pamela held a large umbrella over them while they mounted the stairs to the porch. The old lady was surprisingly agile.

Inside, Granny told them to leave the door open so she could sit in her rocking chair and look at the woods while he built her a fire. He retrieved some kindling and hickory logs from the porch. He arranged the wood amid the ashes of previous fires and enjoyed a pang of anticipation as the sulfur of the match flared before him. When the fire had caught, they arranged Granny Fern before it with a quilt about her. Pamela gave him a tour, insisting he sit on the bed so he could appreciate the feather mattress. She leaned against him and placed her lips against his ear. "I'll bet this is where they did it."

Jewel hurried to his feet and said he was hungry. Pamela pinched his butt as she followed him through the door. Jewel swatted at her hand. "What will your grandmother think?"

The rain drummed on the tin roof as they unpacked the picnic. Just before biting into a deviled egg, Jewel asked Mrs. Ransdell if she had considered his offer on the land. He turned to Pamela and explained the details.

"That's four hundred and fifty thousand dollars. Do you have that kind of money?" Her look indicated a reappraisal of his value to her.

"I can swing it," he said confidently. He didn't bother explaining that he planned on financing the purchase with the timber itself, leaving him the land in the clear.

"Would you give $2,000?" Pamela's eyes narrowed.

"Now wait a damn minute. Who am I dealing with, you or your grandmother?" The words came out more harshly than he had intended, and he laughed to soften their effect.

The old woman tried to speak but began to cough, producing a sound that reminded Jewel of a chainsaw misfiring. Her face took on a frightening shade of red as the fit continued. Finally, she gained control of herself. She wiped her eyes and took a sip of water. "You deal with me," she managed to say though the words sounded as if they had been pressed through a screen.

Jewel hesitated then launched ahead. He said that although he had not seen the entire property that he was willing to adjust his offer on two conditions. One, would they give him their word that what he had seen from the road was indicative of the property as a whole (he knew it was but hoped this strategy would make them trust him more)? Second, that if he agreed to their price that Mrs. Ransdell would sign a contract to be witnessed by Pamela and notarized by him. He always carried contracts in his truck. "In other words, I don't want you just using my price to negotiate another one from someone else if you don't really mean to sell."

A long pause followed. "I'd take $2,000 an acre."

Jewel retrieved a contract and his notary seal from his truck. His heart thumped as he watched the old woman trace her spidery signature across the page. As he signed his own, he felt the elation of a man who has just secured his future. He suggested they all head back to town.

"Not so fast, mister. Granny Fern always has a nap after lunch. Besides, the fire's still going."

"Mrs. Ransdell, do you feel all right? Do you want to lie down?" The high color in the old lady's cheeks worried him, and he would feel safer with Pamela with her grandmother in the bedroom. The old woman shook her head. She stared into the fire intently as if attempting to conjure a vision. But her head soon sagged to her chest while Jewel watched Pamela repack the picnic basket. She looked up and smiled. "Now that Granny's asleep, how's about checking that blind spot?"

~~~

Jewel studied her figure against the window, the weight of her breasts as she fastened her bra. Across the field behind her, a flock of birds scattered from the stand of cottonwoods along the creek. Pamela smiled at him. "I'm not sure how all this is going to work out, but that was just what the doctor ordered."

"Glad I could be of service," Jewel said smugly. This was turning into quite a day. Their coupling had not been at all what he had imagined. Once the bedroom door had closed, she had come at him like a wildcat, ripping his shirt open with a force that removed two buttons. The act itself had been virtually wordless but hardly silent, her shrieks reminding Jewel of those of the pileated woodpecker. She had taken him astraddle while he prayed that Granny Fern was a sound sleeper and wondered when they could leave so he could get to the courthouse and file the contract. He now sat on the edge of the bed holding a cowboy boot.

"Like you didn't want to." She pulled his head against her and tousled his hair. He enjoyed her smell, his cheek pressed to her stomach. "Come on," she said, "we better check on Granny." She went on out while he tugged on his boots and congratulated himself on his superior business skills.

He could hear Pamela calling to her grandmother as he made his way through the house. On the porch, she turned to him with concern. "She's not here."

Why hadn't they strapped her in the chair? He thought of the blackbirds rising from the treeline along the creek, and queasiness rippled through him. "Maybe she walked down toward the woods," he said. Surely she had sense enough not to fall in the creek he thought but did not say or even believe. At the base of the steps, her tracks were clearly defined in the mud, the indentation of the heels resembling small hooves. Though they disappeared as the mud gave way to grass, the direction in which they pointed suggested a tangent that was bound to intersect the creek near the long pool.

If something happened to her, the contract would be worthless at best. He imagined the tract at auction to real estate developers and timber companies, every extra dollar bid coming straight out of his pocket, his future. He broke into a run, scarcely noticing as he slipped and fell, the slick leather soles of his boots providing no purchase against the wet grass. Regaining his feet, he tasted copper and understood that he had bit his tongue. Branches lashed against his face as he plunged into the woods. Pamela's voice registered upon his ears but not his mind, calling for him to wait.

He pushed on, slipped and fell again as he blundered into the shallows like a hunted animal. The swollen creek waters had assumed a clayish hue beneath a froth which drifted above like so many abandoned cobwebs. Up ahead the gray figure of Granny Fern spun slowly, facedown in an eddy as he struggled to his knees, calculating all the while the cost of what lay before him.

The Scrimshaw River

Charles Semones

for **K. C.**

There used to be those nights on the Scrimshaw River,
I remember, when the Full Beaver Moon of November
rose the color of deer-kill and spun in its socket; when
wind-fugues slurred your death, and you still with years to go;
when, root-roiled and moody, I felt beatitudes of flame
stun my tongue, never to be spoken in any human's hearing.

There's no way that a nerve-net's glory can translate
into love I'd hurl across the water to your hunting cabin
where you sprawl nude in my imaginings; no way my mute
desire that's out of joint, unthinkable, can draw you near.
Now there are those November nights on the Scrimshaw River
when the Beaver Moon of deer-kill sets where I'll dig your grave.

Hydrophobia
Patti White

Saturated ground forced the foxes and raccoons out of their dens.
The skunks carried rabies to the feral cats, the feral cats to barn cats,
and finally Velma Jo's kitten attacked her, biting her over the eye,
and then escaped to cause havoc in the barnyard, scattering
chickens, startling the sheep. Inoculations saved her life,
but the disease traveled through the countryside, wild animals
sickening, dropping unnoticed on winter fields.

Weeks later young Charlie Adams grew heavy in the arms,
weak and fatigued, started a fever that ran up like fire
inside a shock of hay, talked anxiously of his wife's milk glass,
rubbed at the scar on his hand, only a scratch, thin, white.

In his hospital bed while the flood raged, shaking,
the sheets soaked with sweat, insects crawling
in his mouth, he refused water, couldn't swallow,
cried out against the cool wet cloth on his forehead

choked on his own saliva, gagging, frothing
the sweat pooled on his skin, his tears scalding.

His family was safe on high ground
the furniture stacked on the second floor
the stock turned out to fend for themselves

his family was safe behind the levee
as he flailed and struggled in a river
rising in his hallucinations, his room
filling with clear water, like his brain

and he fell into a coma as into a well
darkness echoing, a wet grave waiting

and his children, forever after, confused his funeral
with the one they held for the cat, a ragged old tom,
buried in a shoe-box in the cold wet garden, in the rain
that a week later filled the creeks and streams, the river,
and the dens of the foxes, the raccoons, to the brim.

The Frozen Niagara Hotel
Patti White

When the refugees arrived they were stunned
to find Mammoth Cave lit like a wedding cake,
strings of bulbs overhanging the rough stairs
that would take them deep into the earth.

Bedazzled by weeping limestone, they trod
upon a floor iced by generations of rain
and seeping minerals, entered caverns
dreamy with the green glow of lanterns
and the soft brush of bat wings, a land
where the air never varied, always
a cool sweep of mossy breezes flowing
through unseen channels, whispering
to stone twisted into uncanny forms
that would not stand the light of day.

Some, like the children of Hamelin,
would never return, but fall like pebbles
into the emerald river; others awoke
in the hotel lobby, where windows
streamed with rain and fog, a swaying
chandelier above, the tinkling glass
a pattering of water-drops on stone.

For years they told stories no one believed,
tales of stone-blind fish with pale white scales
in lime-laced pools of ink; of mirrored walls
of polished rock, and refugees swallowed
by sink-holes that vanished; of flood-weary
travelers dropping onto soft limestone beds
and sleeping the rain-soaked years away.

Good Girl
Holly Goddard Jones

A YEAR BEFORE Jacob's son, Tommy, was arrested for raping a fifteen-year-old girl, the sheriff came to his shop about the dog. Tommy's dog—a pit bull bitch. Tommy had brought her home the week he graduated from high school, a pup in an old Nike shoe box, eyes just opened. And Jacob had said, "You're not bringing that dog here," but he soon gave in, letting his son keep her on a blanket in the toolshed; weeks later he said, "You're not bringing that dog in the house," but he gave in on that, too, and the dog started sleeping on the living room couch, the same spot where his wife Nora had liked sitting when she was alive.

The one thing he'd stood firm on, he thought at the time, was the treatment of the animal. Tommy wanted her mean, wanted to beat her and chain her to weights and mix gunpowder into her dog food. Jacob wasn't one of those animal rights nut-jobs, and he'd never really liked dogs, or any kind of pet, for that matter—always had to scrub his hands clean after petting one, and even then, he'd go to bed sure that fleas and ticks were crawling all over him, setting up camp in the graying curly hairs of his underarms or groin. But he was softer in his middle age than he'd once been—less casual about life since Nora's passing—and he wouldn't stand back while the poor animal was tortured, made crazy by one of his son's misguided whims. So he'd held firm. He started feeding her when he noticed Tommy was forgetting to, scratching her belly when Tommy was gone and she seemed slow and disconsolate, and at some point—maybe the day he got home from work and she met him at the front porch, bouncing on her hind legs, eyes buggy and worshipful—he realized he loved her, he was grateful to have her. Though he never said so to Tommy, he felt a bittersweet certainty that Nora would have loved her too—good as she'd always been with rough beasts, himself at one time no exception. It was easy, on nights when Tommy slept away and the house felt as open and empty as a tobacco warehouse in January, to imagine the dog as his last connection to Nora. It was a desperate way to feel.

The sheriff was Perry Whitebridge, a good enough old boy. He'd been a year behind Jacob in high school, a soft-spoken kid with duct tape holding his boots together, which wasn't so uncommon in the county back then, when Jacob himself sometimes snacked on wild onions from the side of the road to keep his stomach from rumbling. Jacob ran a gun shop now, and he had a contract with the sheriff's office: they purchased their weapons and ammunition from him at a fair price, and Jacob took care of the cleaning and maintenance of their guns for free. So Jacob had come to know Perry, respected him, and even drank a beer or two with him some nights at the American Legion. Two womanless men: Jacob, a widower, and Perry, just plain unlucky. Or maybe lucky—Jacob knew him, but not well enough to understand how the man felt about those things.

Perry came to the gunshop on a crisp afternoon in early autumn, and Jacob knew from the look on his face that something was up. But he tried to play it normal anyway, thinking Tommy must've been in some trouble, stuck in a situation that would cost Jacob money or face. "Look what the cat dragged in," he said. He wiped the big glass display counter with some Windex and an old rag, looking at his reflection with the guns crisscrossing below it, then up at Perry, who was taking off his hat by the brim with one hand and patting his coarse blond hairs over to one side with the other.

"Got to talk to you, Jake," Perry said.

"Talk, then." *He stole something. A car, maybe. Broke in somewhere. Jesus.*

"This is hard, man." Perry grabbed the counter, putting greasy smears on the glass.

Jacob sighed. "Lay it on me."

"Your dog, Jake. Tommy's dog, I mean. She got into some trouble up the road."

He just about laughed with relief, picturing overturned garbage cans, the contents strewn across a neighbor's yard; a dead rabbit lying on someone's front stoop. "What about her?"

Perry looked at his big hands, then up at Jacob. "She bit someone—that little girl about two miles up from your place, across from the Methodist church."

"The Pryor girl?"

Perry nodded.

Jacob's heart started to beat up in his throat, like reports from a pistol. "Shit. How bad is it?"

"She's gonna be all right," Perry said, and if Jacob had been the crying type, he might have. He'd already seen this girl (Geena? Jenny?) in his head—dark haired and wild, always wearing a ring of dirt round her neck like a piece of jewelry—mangled, pretty dark eyes ripped from their sockets. He knew the power in that dog; when they played, and Jacob teased her with the thick hank of rope with the knot tied in the end of it, she just about ripped his arm out of the socket trying to yank it free.

"Yeah, it could've been worse," Perry said. "The dog bore down on her leg pretty hard, but down on the calf where there's more meat. Mrs. Pryor had to whack her upside the head with a shovel to knock her loose, long enough to get the kid inside. She called me, but the dog was gone by time I got out there."

"What should I do?"

Perry's face was shiny. "I'm supposed to get the dog warden out to your place, have her put down. That's what I'm supposed to do. And the family could press charges against you."

"Shit," Jacob said.

Perry leaned in. "They're good folks, though, and the little girl's gonna be all right, like I said. You give them some money for their bills and a little bit extra, they'll let it go. And do something about that dog. Pen her up, send her to your cousin's in Timbuktu, whatever. I don't know. I'm willing to let this one slide, Jake. Dogs go funny every now and then. Just don't make me regret it."

Jacob shook his hand. "I'm grateful, man. I mean it. And you won't regret it."

Perry smiled, the lines in the corners of his eyes folded like a stack of clean towels. "No, I'm sure I won't."

Jacob closed the shop right after Perry left and drove straight home. Tommy was gone, of course; he worked fifteen or twenty hours a week for a construction company out of Springfield, Tennessee, spent the rest of his time either fucking that girl he was seeing—Leela, who was twenty-six and had three kids already and a loose fold of stretch-marked skin that hung over the top of her low-slung jeans, but at least had her tubes tied—or getting fucked up with his work buddies, pot or beer, whatever they could get cheaper that day. Jacob was lucky to get a meal in with the kid once a week, and even then he often had to tempt him with something nicer, like Ponderosa. He realized that he should probably put Tommy out of the house for a while, make him scrape up a living on his own—he was nineteen now, and Jacob was making it too easy for him to waste what little he made on cigarettes and alcohol—but he couldn't do it. Just couldn't. The living was lonely since Nora passed, and Jacob walked around with the dread, the looming possibility of a life by himself in his little house in the country: watching reruns of *Bonanza* every night on television, eating pork and beans straight out of the can, not bothering to heat them up. Seeing Nora's shadow in her garden in the backyard, now two seasons overgrown; her cool shoulder turning away from him in bed. Tommy was gone already, mostly, but Jacob would miss the smell of the boy's cologne, his white athletic socks balled in dirty wads on the living room floor. Even his tired eyes—hungover, yes, but dark brown like his mother's—glancing up from the plate of sausage and toast Jacob cooked up for him on Sunday mornings.

The dog was waiting for him on the front porch, wagging her tail. "Good girl," Jacob whispered, bending down on his bad knee to scratch behind her ears, under her chin. She was an ugly animal—face broad and stupid, fur rust-colored and mottled, like granite. Tommy had gotten her ears clipped when she was still small, and they stood up on top of her head, two triangles of flesh, pink-lined like seashells. But her body was long and smooth, sculpted, and Jacob traced the line of muscle that defined her back haunches, marveling as always at such wild, stealthy beauty it frightened him. She licked the palm of his hand.

"Good lady," he said.

He went into his house, to his bedroom, and opened the closet door. There was a safe in the bottom, under a pile of clothes and shoes that Jacob swept unceremoniously to the side. He turned the dial right, left, right again. What he had, the little he had, was inside: a stack of E series savings bonds, maybe twenty thousand dollars' worth; his grandmother's collection of silver dollars; the deed on the house; and the gun he'd saved for years to buy, even before he knew if he'd find it: a Colt .45 pistol, still in its original box, with the original screwdriver for disassembling. He had the papers: Issued by the Army in 1911, carried by a soldier in World War I, a fellow named Hughbert Waltham. Jacob had paid nearly four thousand dollars for it at a gun show in Nashville, a bargain he'd considered too good to be believed; he could get at least six thousand for it now, probably more. He thought about the Pryor girl. He would need every penny.

The bullets were in a cardboard box in the back of the safe. Jacob took a seat on his bed near the window, where he could see better, and pulled out one. His .38 was in the drawer by his bedside table, loaded, but that wasn't the gun for this job. You had to know the right gun for the job, he believed. The clip was empty. He thumbed the safety, pulled back the slide with his left hand, holding the walnut grip with his right; then he shifted hands and inserted the bullet into the chamber. The gun gleamed in the afternoon light. Jacob looked forward to cleaning it, using the tiny screwdriver, handling the parts with a soft cloth on the velvet-covered surface of his work bench. He took the magazine in his right hand again, grasping the slide with his left, and depressed the trigger halfway, easing the slide into place. He would do this outside, normally, but the dog would hear and know. He didn't want her to know anything.

She sat on the porch with her back to the door, facing the road. She turned when Jacob came outside, storm door clanging behind him, and his hidden hand would have set her on alert with any other human, but she trusted him. He patted her hide and made a clicking sound in the back of his throat, signaling her to heel, and she followed him to the backyard.

This was the shame: a dog was a dog, Jacob knew, and they weren't born to hurt little girls, only raised to be that way. And he'd turned his face away too many times when Tommy played rough, smacking the dog across the jaw with an empty two-liter bottle, shoving her off the front porch with a steel-toed work boot. It wasn't this one's fault. It was his, for being too weak to stand up to his own son and tell him right from wrong. She'd been a good dog to Jacob, a sweet girl, a protector. He bent over and stroked her back, the short, bristly hairs there, and she sat up, alert, watching the woods behind his property with her intelligent and predatory gaze. He thumbed the safety off the gun, lifted it up to the back of her head, and pulled the trigger.

She fell over, a dark heap in high grass.

Jacob buried her in Nora's garden and waited up until almost four in the morning for Tommy to get back. He explained about the girl and what the dog had done to her, how a bullet was cheaper than a lawsuit. "And once a dog gets human blood in her mouth, she'll never lose the taste for it," he finished. "That's what my own daddy said, anyway." He watched Tommy's face, hoping for a sign that he understood his own stake in what happened without Jacob spelling it out for him. He was a good-looking boy, short— barely five foot seven—but wiry, with dark eyes and skin and hair, like a Mexican, almost. He stretched, his "Hank 3" shirt pulling out of his gray jogging pants, and patted Jacob's shoulder on the way to his bedroom.

"No biggie, Pop," he said. The "Pop" thing was new, two months, maybe. "I had my eye out for something different, anyhow." He went to bed, and Jacob again allowed himself a moment to suspect—to hope, really—that Tommy was just playing tough, hiding the hurt he felt.

Jacob stayed up another hour, working Fill Em In's at the kitchen table— "the soulless crossword," Nora had called them whenever Jacob picked up a new copy from the magazine rack at the Piggly Wiggly. He liked the mindlessness of finding an intersection for random words and numbers, all the information you needed in front of you, no clues or guesswork required. He finished one, his eyes weak in the low light, back burning from hunching over so long without moving. He traced his fingers over the surface of the page, the indentations of his ballpoint pen. He reached down to touch the dog, where she would normally have been sleeping beside him, and the emptiness of his life registered in full and aching force. "Nora," he said, looking at her shadow figure on the old living room couch—head bent over one of the mysteries she loved reading, Agatha Christie or Anne Rule— dark, shoulder-length hair glinting in the lamplight. She lifted her head at the sound of his voice, took off her glasses, smiled. Her face, the face she wore before the embolism and her death: gentle, intelligent, elegantly lined, like crackled pottery.

~~~

   Three months before Jacob's son was arrested for raping the Winterson girl, Jacob saw Helen for the first time. He was eating lunch alone at Gary's Pit Barbecue on the bypass and thinking about how strange it was to see two nicely dressed women—one quite young, early twenties maybe, the other closer to his own age—eating thick-piled pork barbecue sandwiches between spurts of typing on their laptops. He liked it. He wasn't a man who adapted well to change, and he probably couldn't even figure out how to turn one of those things on, but there was something reassuring about this picture, nonetheless: the mix of old and new, the idea that his hometown could move on in some ways and stay the same where it counted. He squeezed some hot sauce on his sandwich and took a big bite, still watching them, and the older woman looked up and caught his eye. His mouth was full of spicy meat and the sour tang of sauce, but he swallowed fast and smiled.
   She smiled back, then turned her gaze down to the screen.
   She was a handsome woman—that's how Jacob's mother would have put it—with gray hair, shortly cropped, styled. Nice hair: not yellow-gray like Jacob's was turning, but striking and pure, as if she'd been born with it that way. He couldn't tell her eye color from here, but it was something light, blue or hazel, and she had a fine, thin nose with the slightest upturn at the tip. She was a professional of some kind, he figured—an administrator at the hospital, maybe a lawyer. He guessed it said something else about the way the town was changing, that he didn't know who she was, what she did for a living. He liked that, too.
   He finished his meal and left a ten-dollar bill on the table, held down by a shaker of Lawry's. He caught his waitress's eye across the restaurant—Rita, her boy had gone to school with Tommy—and pointed at the table. She nodded and lifted a hand.
   The air outside was always a surprise after the smells of the restaurant: the fried batters, the fragrant burn of wood smoke. From the entrance Jacob could see the bypass—a newly blacktopped slash through what had once been the Brindle farm—wooded on this side, lined with trailers on the other. He reflected on another smell in the restaurant, one he'd breathed in as he crossed the dining room to the door, past the portraits of Adolph Rupp and Rick Pitino and the photos of the state championship football

team from 1987: women's perfume, an unnameable sweetness, freshening the other scents but not drowning them. The memory of the smell excited him, made the closely clipped hairs at the base of his neck rise. He hadn't felt this way in a long time. He'd dated since Nora's death—two or three times, all setups that ended comfortably but without event—and he'd seen women on TV who struck him as sexy, arousing him so abruptly that he felt almost hijacked. Six months ago he drove to the adult bookstore on 65 and purchased a porn video that he pulled out from under his bed sometimes when Tommy was gone to Leela's. Watching it left him stirred but empty.

When he met Nora—that was over thirty years ago, hard as it was to believe—he'd been twenty-five and reckless as hell, more interested in where the next shot of Jack was coming from than whether or not he'd be alive the next day to feel hungover. And the sex then was like the drinking: powerful but singular, a disorienting night trip that left him wrung out and slimy feeling, so that the only thing he hated worse the next day than himself was the girl who gave it up to him so easily and thoughtlessly. Then he met Nora—sweet Nora, who'd only been with one man, one time, and regretted it deeply—and it didn't take him long to realize he loved her, and he wanted her. Before they slept together for the first time, he told her about the other girls— "whores," he called them, "cheap whores." And she hadn't disagreed.

He pulled out his keys, ready to cross the parking lot to his Chevy diesel and drive back to work. But the smell of perfume was still in his nose, making him lightheaded. He turned, went back through the door, and crossed the dining room to her table. There was a deer head mounted to a plaque on the opposite wall, and he felt it staring at him through the dark-tinted sunglasses someone had balanced on its nose as a joke. The young girl noticed him first, drawing her eyebrows together—wary, as if he might be trying to sell her something. The older woman stopped typing on her computer and merely smiled: the kind of smile, Jacob thought, that the loan officer had given him the first time he came in about opening the gun shop. He felt now much like he had felt then: inadequate, ridiculous for dreaming. He almost fled.

"Yes?" she asked.

"You're new," he said, neck hot. "I mean, you seem new. To town."

"I am new," she said. Were her cheeks a little pink? He thought so. "I moved down here about a month ago."

"What brought you?" Jacob asked. And it wasn't just the deer's eyes that he felt on him now; Rita, the waitress, was watching him over the pitcher of sweet tea she was carrying to a booth. Smiling, Jacob was sure. And the old men at the next table were certainly slowing down their conversation about the upcoming mayor's race.

The woman grabbed her briefcase from an adjacent chair and dug around, pulling out a business card tweezed between two lacquered fingers. Her picture was in the corner, her name beneath it: "Helen Shively, CRS, GRI." To the left was a logo he recognized: "Campbell L. Baldwin & Sons Real Estate and Auctioneers, serving Logan County since 1929."

"You're an agent?"

"Yep," she said. " Just getting started. So if you know anybody shopping around for a house—" She shrugged a little and laughed. A nice laugh.

"Maybe I do," Jacob lied. "I'll ask around."

"That would be great," Helen said.

Jacob looked from Helen to her friend and angled his body toward Helen. He lowered his voice. "If you'd like someone to show you around, I have a shop in town. You could stop by. Not that there's much to show. Hell, you've been here a month. I guess you've seen it all."

Helen laughed again. "Probably have," she said. "But we could have a coffee sometime anyway."

"A coffee," Jacob said. "Sure. Sure."

She nodded toward his hand. "You have my card."

"Yeah," Jacob said. "I do." He smiled now, and feeling his face that way he was suddenly aware of how rarely he smiled anymore. "Thanks for that."

"You're welcome," Helen said, and though it was hardly in his nature, Jacob thought he'd call her. He thought she wanted him to.

Outside, letting the wind cool his flushed cheeks, he rubbed his thumb across the raised lettering of her card. Helen—he remembered that name from the baby books he'd looked at with Nora, one of the times she was pregnant. It hadn't made their final list of girl's names, but he'd liked it, because the book had told a story about a face that launched a thousand ships, a woman so beautiful that men lost their heads. "If you want to set your expectations so high," Nora had said, "let's call her Athena. I'd rather have smart than pretty." And Jacob had agreed.

Now that the fear was behind him, the excitement returned—a warm fist in his belly, clenching, releasing. He climbed into his truck and tucked Helen's card into the visor, where he wouldn't lose it. He closed his eyes and recalled her face, memorizing it, not wanting to lose that either. Helen. He started the car and pulled out of the parking lot, heading back to his shop.

~~~

Later he'd recall how it felt to love a woman again. Because it seemed
to Jacob that a life only had room for so many beautiful things, even if you
were lucky: a true love, a healthy child, a job that you could wake up to
each day with even faint anticipation. That Helen could see something in
him—perhaps the same thing Nora knew lay beneath the bourbon-scented
sweat of the day labor he hated—struck him as somehow miraculous. A
miracle. The miracle of a good woman.

~~~

On a Saturday morning in early November, Perry's cruiser pulled into
Jacob's driveway. Jacob was on the front porch having a swing, thinking
about meeting Helen in town for ice cream and a drive; right now the days
were still brisk and eye-wateringly sunny, but the air was already getting
that bitter smell. In another week or so he'd need to take down the swing
for the winter and stow it in the garage, under a tarp, so that the boards
wouldn't warp with cold and moisture.

Tommy hadn't made it home last night. Jacob didn't even let Tommy's
absences keep him up anymore; he gave himself over to thin, uneasy sleep
instead, dreaming with such frantic energy that he usually awoke feeling jit-
tery and out of touch. He financed a cellular phone that his son had never
used once to call home. Twice he'd determined to let the bill slip and the
service disconnect; twice he'd paid the bill by phone on the day it was due,
picking up a five-dollar surcharge for his trouble. He was in awe of his own
weakness; he hardly recognized himself anymore.

Jacob had the sense, watching Perry Whitebridge exit his car and begin
a slow stride up the front walk, of reliving a nightmare; it reminded him of
the way he had felt on waking each morning in the first few months after
Nora's death, sure that she was still in the bed beside him, or in the kitchen
starting coffee, the sureness somehow accompanied by a feeling of depres-
sion and doom. That moment before the two things—the sureness and the
doom—came together to make sense of one another, almost worse than
the despair that inevitably followed, and the glimmer of hope in the drawer
of his bedside table, the .38 that he would surely have used if there hadn't
been Tommy to think on and love and worry about, Tommy to hear the
gunshot from his bed in the next room.

*Car accident. Drinking and driving. He killed someone. He's dead. Please god,
someone else, not Tommy. Please god, not Tommy.*

Perry stopped at the front step, hesitant. "Need to have a talk with you, Jake," he said.

"Talk, then," Jacob told him.

~~~

The day Tommy had started kindergarten—his small arms dangling out of the short sleeves of his new plaid button-down shirt, both hands clutching the handle of his plastic Teenage Mutant Ninja Turtles lunch box—Nora had returned to her job at the nursing home. Jacob had warned her against taking on too many big changes all at once, but she'd been adamant. "I can't stand sitting around that house all day by myself," she told him. "I'd have the house cleaned by lunchtime, then I'd spend the rest of the day watching TV or taking naps."

It hadn't just been that, though, and Jacob knew it. She missed the work. Tommy was late for a first child—Nora had miscarried four times before his birth, and she was thirty-eight when she delivered him—so she had adjusted to motherhood with difficulty as well as joy. When he was crawling age, she started making trips to the home to visit the residents, not worried like Jacob was about what germs the baby might pick up. The old people had loved touching the boy, planting dry, shaky kisses on his bald head. He never got sick, though. Not from them, not even a bad cold.

In the car, driving Tommy home from a night in lock-up, Jacob remembered what it was like to have a small, happy son. Random memories: He, Nora, and Tommy picnicking at Lake Malone, Jacob sipping on a Keystone and watching Tommy in the water, buoyant in his Mickey Mouse arm floaties; Tommy graduating from kindergarten, chewing on the tassel dangling from his white cap instead of singing "The Bear Went Over the Mountain" with his classmates; Tommy asleep in the middle of the living room floor wearing only a diaper, the ceiling fan creaking above him and cooling his round cheeks, red-flushed from hard play. Pain raced through Jacob's arm and he grabbed it, sucking air through his teeth.

"Dad, you okay?"

"Fine," Jacob said.

"Don't be a hero, man. Let's get you to the doctor if you're going to have a heart attack or something."

Jacob pulled the car over onto the shoulder, unlatched his seatbelt, and backhanded Tommy with his good arm. Tommy's head knocked against the passenger-side window, hard, but he had the good sense not to say anything in return, only to sit there, slack jawed and wide eyed, pawing at his red-and-white blotched cheek.

"You've had that coming for a while," Jacob said. He closed his eyes and kneaded the tight spot in his chest. There was a moment when the pain seemed ready to cross over from bad to serious, and Jacob could even hear that *wonk! wonk!* sound in his head that always announced DANGER in the movies. Then it started to subside. He took deep breaths, massaged, opened his eyes. A few seconds later, he noticed the road ahead of him, where Les Clemmons's row of neatly kept board fence ran out into Paul Brown's scraggly old barbed wire contraption; the Presbyterian church up on the hill to the left, where one of his uncles was buried.

"Dad?" Tommy whispered.

Jacob looked at the church, wondered whether he could see the boneyard from here if he strained hard enough. There was a spot of white under a big tree.

"Daddy, you've got me scared."

Jacob reached across Tommy and opened the glove box. The bottle of aspirin was stuffed behind the owner's manual, and Jacob shook two out; he chewed them dry, the bitter taste drawing him out of his fog.

"I'm okay." He meant it, he felt better. As with the two previous times this had happened—once at work, once just after Nora's funeral—he felt almost silly after the pain passed, as if he'd been imagining the whole thing, or exaggerating it. There had been a moment, when Jacob was just about Tommy's age, when he looked in the mirror, hardened the big muscles in his chest and arms, and thought, *My lord, I'm iron.* Two seconds of clarity and beauty, nothing more, but he never forgot them. How awful to know that kind of sureness in your life, only to lose it.

He started the car, refastened his seatbelt.

"I can pay you back the bond money," Tommy was saying. "I'll sell the truck if I have to. I've got this covered."

"A lawyer's gonna cost a lot more than a thousand dollars," Jacob said.

"I'll figure it out." He lit a cigarette and cracked a window, letting the wind catch the ashes and pull them out of the car. "They'll set you up on payments. I know a guy."

"I'm sure you do."

"Got Chad off a DUI. He only charged five hundred."

"This is a hell of a lot more serious than a goddamned DUI," Jacob said. "Christ almighty, Tommy, I thought you had more sense. I thought your mother had raised you better."

"So that's it? Somebody says I did something, you right off believe them? Real nice, Dad. Not that I'd expect any different."

They pulled into the driveway and Jacob shut off the car.

"Well, you tell me, then," Jacob said. "Did you hurt that girl?"

"No," Tommy said. His hand, the one grabbing for the door handle, was shaking. "Of course I didn't."

"You going to call this lawyer, or do I have to do that, too? The arraignment's on Monday."

"I'll call him, Dad. Jesus."

Jacob rubbed his mouth, his dry lips, and thought about Helen for the first time since yesterday, when Perry came. "I wonder about you, Tom," he said. He looked at his son, who was staring off in the direction of Nora's overrun garden where the dog was buried and playing with the flip top on the ash tray. "I just wonder."

"Don't," Tommy said.

Jacob left it at that.

~~~

Tommy was gone until the morning of the arraignment—Springfield again, spending the weekend with Leela, and Jacob hadn't had the energy to argue—so Helen came over Sunday night, bringing with her some cobbler and a bottle of Maker's. While Jacob gave her the details about Tommy's arrest, she searched his cabinets for food, then started cooking grilled cheese sandwiches and chicken noodle soup, her movements fluid and efficient—the way she could butter the bread without tearing it, or flip the sandwiches in the pan with one fast motion that didn't shift the corners. Before Helen, he hadn't had a woman cook for him—for him and only him—in almost three years. He'd missed too many other things about Nora, important things, to allow himself to grieve for something as selfish as this, but he grieved for it now: the gift of a meal you didn't make yourself.

"I wasn't much older than Tommy when Nora and me got married," Jacob told Helen, watching her work. She knew this—she knew most of what there was worth knowing about him, he was sure—but he needed to say it again. To make sense of it.

"Me, too," Helen said. "It was a different time." She had, Jacob learned in the two and a half months of their careful courtship, married when she was twenty, divorced twenty years later. It wasn't something she often talked about, but his name was Harry, she'd told him, he drove trucks for Overnite, and *he* left *her*—not for a twenty-five-year-old "slip of ass," which she could just about have understood, she'd said, but for a lawyer seven years his senior down in San Antonio.

"It's not just the difference in age," Jacob said. He poured another shot of bourbon into his coffee mug, grateful for the warmth. Nora had never fussed when Jacob drank but didn't like being around him when he did, and she would've died before going out and purchasing a bottle of whiskey herself. "Marrying settled me somehow. These kids don't ever figure that out. I sure wasn't born a good man."

"But you are one," Helen said.

"If am, it's because Nora made me that way."

Helen stopped stirring the soup and sighed. "Goddamn, Jacob, you sure give a girl a lot to live up to."

She'd said things like this before, and hearing her jealousy—there wasn't a better word for it—always surprised him. Nora was as much a part of his life as his son. He could stop talking about her—thinking about her—no better than he could stop breathing.

"Don't mean anything by it," he said into his drink. And though he didn't feel his comment had warranted an apology, he offered one: "Sorry. I'm sorry, hon."

"No need," Helen said. She sighed again—he didn't even think she was aware of doing it—and stirred the soup more vigorously.

He hadn't eaten much of anything since Perry came by with his news—drank coffee, nibbled on a bear claw he got out of a vending machine at the police station—so he indulged himself now, putting away two sandwiches and two helpings of soup, plus a slab of the blackberry cobbler drenched in some of the vanilla ice cream Helen had found in the back of his freezer. He washed the dinner dishes while Helen read a magazine, and then they made love—not for the first time, of course, but it was still new, and Jacob had never felt so satisfied, so frankly grateful to another human being. He didn't love Helen like he'd loved his wife, but he did love her, and he said so.

He was close to sleep when she rolled over and worked her way between his arm and side, resting her head on his chest. "There's a house," she said, her own voice soft and sleepy. "Right outside of Auburn. It's going on the market in a few weeks."

"Yeah?" he said, moving his feet into a cooler pocket of sheet.

"Yeah." Her breath hit his nipple, sending a chill down his back. "It's a nice place, Jake, part of an estate. The kids are in a hurry to close and split the sale money."

He was awake now. "So what are you saying?"

"I'm buying it, Jake." Her finger traced the line of his ribcage. "I want you to live with me there. I want us to get it together."

He didn't say anything, couldn't. What about Tommy? Tommy wasn't part of this plan, he was sure.

"Don't worry about it now," Helen said. She stretched and rolled away, because they'd both figured out that they didn't sleep well in each other's arms. "It was a bad time to mention it. But the offer's there."

"I'll think on it," Jacob said.

"That's all I'm asking."

But it wasn't all she was asking, he knew. And when she fell asleep beside him, the same place his wife had slept when she was alive, he went to Tommy's room, sat on his son's bed, and wondered if Helen wasn't trying to strip him of the little he had left of Nora—killing her again with softness and warmth and the possibility of something new and alive.

~~~

Perry Whitebridge called Jacob on the evening following the arraignment, asked him if they could meet somewhere. Tommy, for the first time since Jacob had picked him up from the county lockup, was quiet, morose. He sat in front of the television after dinner, not bothering to flip the channel, and ate from a bag of Reeses peanut butter cups left over from Halloween. A pile of brown paper wrappers spilled off the edge of the end table and littered the carpet, crinkled and twisted like dead leaves.

"Well, I guess you're scared now," Jacob had told him, driving home from court. A mean thing to say, he knew, and ironic, considering: Jacob himself had found the arraignment much less intimidating than he'd worried it would be, schooled as he was in episodes of *Law and Order*. Tommy hadn't even had to say anything: he just sat there while the judge outlined the charges, and it was his lawyer who called out "not guilty." The Winterson girl—the victim, they'd called her—wasn't even there. That was what had worried Jacob more than anything: seeing this girl his son was supposed to have hurt.

"Of course I'm scared," Tommy had said. Then he started to cry, high-pitched hitches that shocked Jacob so badly he almost ran the car into the shoulder. He went ahead and slowed to a stop, unlatching his seatbelt. Tommy shrank back when he put his arms out, but Jacob grabbed him roughly anyway, pulling him to his shoulder, and Tommy shook in his arms while he thrummed an awkward, consoling rhythm on Tommy's back. And just as he was reminded of how much he loved this boy, this piece of himself—more fiercely than he'd ever loved anyone, even Nora—he understood that Tommy had done something to that girl, and that the hurting was maybe only just starting.

"Well, I'm here," Jacob had said, patting, feeling both comforted and repulsed by the warmth of his son's back. "There's that."

Jacob and Perry arranged to meet at a truck stop in Bowling Green—a thirty-minute ride from home, but Perry had insisted on getting out of town, and Jacob hadn't wanted to question him. He was hunched over a mug of coffee when Jacob arrived, blowing the liquid between quick sips. He stood when Jacob approached the booth, and they shook hands, strangely formal in a way that Jacob didn't understand.

"Have a sit," Perry said, and he did.

"I haven't been here before," Jacob told him. "Cozy."

"Yeah, it's all right." Perry tapped a beat on the scratched laminate of the tabletop—"Shave and a Haircut," it sounded like. "I come here now and then."

They looked at each other. An eighteen-wheeler roared to life outside, and they both jumped a little.

"Well, Christ," Perry said. "I'll get right to it."

"What?"

"It's one of those good news and bad news things. I'll give you the bad first, okay?"

"Okay," Jacob said.

Perry leaned in. "There's a couple of witnesses, say they saw Tommy picking the girl up in his truck down by Sonic the night she says it happened."

Jacob nodded, rubbing his face.

"I talked to this one kid, off the cuff, so to speak. He told me this girl, this Winterson girl, she worked at Sonic Thursdays and Fridays, and Tommy had an eye on her. Always parked in her section."

Jacob waited.

"Well, you see where I'm going with this."

"Yeah," Jacob said. "Yeah, I do."

"I'm sorry, man," Perry whispered.

Jacob put his hand over his eyes, noticing how the bright fluorescents made the edges of his skin glow orange, like a jack-o-Lantern.

"There's good news, remember."

"Let's hear it," Jacob said hoarsely.

"There's a process for all this, you know," Perry said. "The grand jury's the next step. That date got set, right?"

"January," Jacob told him.

"All right, then. Well, the commonwealth attorney has to prove to the jury that there's sufficient evidence to try the case. If he can't—or if he doesn't—they'll throw it out."

Jacob's heart started to beat so hard that he was sure Perry could hear it. "What's this mean?"

"Where do you think the attorney gets his evidence from, Jake?"

Jacob exhaled in a rush, his face hot, peppery feeling. "You wouldn't be willing to. You wouldn't—"

Perry put his hand up. "Hold up just a second. Let's be straight. I'm not going to lie about anything. Next year's an election year."

Jacob made a fist under the table, trying to push all of his anger into it. Just as soon as he'd allowed himself to feel hopeful he understood that this was Perry's game, and the little divide between them—the things he hadn't known, hadn't wanted to know—was deep, and much darker than he'd figured. But how little had he known his own son? How much did he really even know himself?

"What I'm willing to do is talk to the commonwealth attorney," Perry said. "He takes my word on things. If I say back off, he probably will. Can't guarantee it, but I'd bet on it."

"Why would you do that?" Jacob asked.

"Hell, Jake, we go back."

"Still."

Perry shrugged and pulled back from the table. "These girls. I don't know, man. They're different nowadays. Time was, a girl knew what she should and shouldn't do. You know what I'm saying?"

Jacob, not sure if he did, nodded.

"She got in the truck with him, that's what I mean. And I heard things about her from that kid, the one who told me about Tommy. He said that she hangs out at the Sonic after her shift ends, smoking and drinking and all that shit. Fifteen, I mean Christ."

"Fifteen," Jacob echoed.

"A good girl just don't do that. Good girls know better. Maybe it was mutual and maybe it wasn't. Either way it's tough to prove. How old is Tommy again?"

"He's twenty," Jacob said.

"Well you see, that's already something. Another year and they could've got him on third-degree rape, and that's at much as a five-year sentence."

Too many ages, numbers. Jacob couldn't think.

"This one wouldn't fly, Jakey. Not likely, anyway. It's her word against his, and like I said, her word ain't so respectable from what I've heard."

"I don't know," Jacob said *Jakey*. His father had called him Jakey.

"What don't you know?" Perry pulled a pack of Camels from his shirt pocket and lit one. "All I'll do is push the commonwealth attorney a little. Make sure he does what he'd probably do anyway. Tommy's learned his lesson, I bet. There's no sense in his life getting ruined over this."

Jacob wondered what Nora would say. But if Nora were still alive, this wouldn't ever have happened.

"You're a good man, Perry," Jacob said, feeling like a liar.

"Hell, buddy. So are you."

~~~

Katie. That was her first name, Tommy had told him. Katie Winterson.

Jacob watched, truck parked in the back of the lot, away from the order intercoms. There looked to be three waitresses on duty: one older, late-thirties probably, and two teenagers. He felt, for no reason in particular, that she must be the smaller of the two—one of those too-tiny types in clunky shoes, breasts like dumplings, dishwater blonde hair in pigtails that bobbed against her thin shoulders. She carried a tray full of white fast food baggies out to a mini-van, balanced it on her hip, counted out change from a metal dispenser belted around her waist. She didn't look beaten, or traumatized. She didn't look happy, either.

A half hour before closing, he pulled into a slot and ordered something called an Arctic Slush. The older waitress brought it out. It looked like Windex, tasted like watery toothpaste. He got out of his truck and pitched it into a wastebasket.

At eleven the lights around the intercoms dimmed, and the Sonic sign shut off. A few teenagers hung out in the parking lot playing music out of souped-up speaker systems, their cars seeming to hover over neon-tinted light effects that struck Jacob as somehow mystical and horrifying. A sedan pulled up to the back door at eleven-thirty, and the girl—Katie, he was sure it must be Katie—exited the restaurant moments later, climbing into the passenger front seat. There was a moment, when her door was open and the dome light flared, when Jacob could see everything: the middle-aged woman behind the wheel, a dog—some kind of lab mix—putting his nose into the front seat, Katie turning to put her face into his, rubbing the scruff behind his ears. Then her door slammed, and the car was dark again. He watched it pull out and drive away.

A week after Tommy's arrest, Jacob drove out past Auburn, following the instructions Helen had written for him in her old-fashioned script: *Two miles after crossroads, turn left at the red barn. Drive out five more miles. House down gravel drive on R, just past Presb. church. Red brick w/ brown shingles.* She would meet him there, she'd said. She had a busy week, houses to show in Auburn and Lewisburg, plus a trip to Bowling Green that afternoon to sign papers. He hadn't seen her in a few days, and he already missed her.

Her car was parked in the drive when he arrived, and Jacob pulled in beside it. The house was larger than he'd imagined it would be, nicer. It was a full two stories, cottage-style, with a wood door and shutters and a roof that looked like it needed some repair, but not much. Shade trees lined the drive, and the backyard sloped down into a thicket of evergreens and brush, the kind of dense growth Tommy would have called a jungle when he was younger. Most of the leaves had fallen from the trees, and they made a thick carpet around the house. As he walked the grounds, looking for Helen, he was reminded of a trip he and Nora had taken to the Biltmore Estate in North Carolina. This would have been about ten years ago. Nora had remarked that the forest looked like a fairy tale forest: tall trees making a canopy high overhead, neat, unlittered ground surrounding them. No weeds, no snarls of kudzu or scrawny saplings. That forest had been carefully pruned and manicured by a whole team of day laborers, but this little grove was merely quiet, untouched.

"So what do you think?" Helen called from behind him.

"Not too bad," he said, crossing the yard to hug her. Her gray hair was tucked behind her ear on one side, and he kissed the silky bit of skin just south of her earlobe, breathing in where she'd dotted her perfume—White Shoulders, he knew now, an old bottle she'd made last. His breath hitched a little in his chest, and he felt a kind of wistful ache he'd felt at other times in his life: once, when he was eleven, watching from across the yard as his father leaned easily against the back fence row, cleaning his fingernails with a pocketknife; also later, driving his first car through the countryside and thinking that life would never be so good again.

"Do you want to see the inside?"

He didn't know. Did he want to see this kitchen he and Helen would eat dinner together in, or the living room where they'd watch television, the sound getting louder as the both of them got deafer? Did he want to see the bathroom where he'd hang the antique shaving mirror Nora had bought him for their fifth anniversary? Or the toolshed he'd putter around in after he sold the gunshop and retired? Did he want to see the master suite, this bedroom he and Helen would share for the next twenty years, maybe more, first making love, then simply sleeping, and maybe, finally, Helen tucking pillows behind his head so he could eat the soup she was spoon-feeding him, catching dribbles with a napkin before they fell off his chin and landed on his flannel pajama top? Could he imagine a life where Nora was just another memory?

"Maybe we should just sit here for a minute," he said, motioning to the front stoop.

"It's kind of cold," Helen said.

"I'll keep you warm."

They sat side by side, Helen leaning into his chest, and Jacob took the left side of his big quilted coat and pulled it around her, shielding her face from the wind.

"Sixty-five thousand," she said, her voice muffled. "I mean, I just couldn't believe it at first. The twenty acres alone are worth that."

"Kind of late for starting over, don't you think?"

"I have some money left over from selling the house with Harry," Helen said. Her hand brushed the bare skin between his shirt tail and work pants, chilling him. "I could mortgage the rest easy, get it paid down in five years or less. Or you could put up the other half."

"I have a house," Jacob said. Her touch was so cold it seared.

"But there're so many memories attached to that place."

"Maybe I want my memories," he said.

"I never said you had to give up your memories."

They watched a gust of wind pick up a pile of leaves, swirling them.

"What about Tommy?"

"You don't have to give him up, either." She exhaled, her breath frosting a current of air. "But he's a big boy, Jacob. He has to move on with his life at some point. And so do you."

"You're saying he wouldn't have a place here, then," Jacob said.

"I'm saying he shouldn't."

When Jacob was young—high school-age—this woman down the street from him had stroked. She was young, too, he knew now—early forties, probably, an age that had seemed impossible to him at the time; still, watching what the stroke had done to her—twisting her face ("handsome," his mother had said. "She was a handsome woman"), turning her into something witchlike—was terrifying. This woman's husband had stayed with her, but a few years after the stroke he was seeing other women, and before too much time had passed one of these women was living in the house, too. Quite the scandal. Jacob's mother was up in arms, but his father, in his quiet way, had only said, "There's lots of ways to love, son," and that had made more sense to him at the time than his mother's yelling and flapping of dishtowels. There *were* lots of ways to love, he thought now—ways that made you a better person than you were, maybe, and ways that got you through lonely times, and also ways, he figured, that could destroy you if you let them. So many ways to love a woman, but only one way to love a child, and that was the single thing he felt sure about anymore.

"I guess I won't be coming in," he told Helen, holding his coat tight around them both, wanting to keep her under his arm for as long as possible. She didn't say anything. He could feel her warm breath through his shirt, and he held her tighter.

~~~

A little over three months after Jacob's son raped Katie Winterson, Jacob and Tommy ate dinner together at Ponderosa. He had a coupon he'd clipped from the newspaper—sirloin tip dinner with salad bar for $6.99, limit four persons per coupon. The grand jury had met two weeks earlier and dismissed the charges, just as Perry had told Jacob they would. He hadn't seen much of Tommy since, between work and the time Tommy was spending with that woman in Springfield.

"I'm starving," Tommy said, grabbing a plastic plate from a stack at the end of the buffet. While Jacob put a salad together, Tommy made two trips back and forth to the table, salad on the first plate, chicken wings, mashed potatoes, a slice of pizza, and two dinner rolls on the other. There'd been a time when Jacob could eat like that, never gain a pound. Like so many things in his life, that time had passed.

They ate silently, Jacob working through his salad, wincing at the metallic taste of the processed bacon bits, then his sirloin tips, dipped in a puddle of A-1. Tommy's chicken wings, stripped free of meat and breading and even cartilage, piled up on a saucer in the middle of the table. A waitress refilled their glasses of sweet tea a few times, and Tommy finished with a saucer full of soft serve ice cream, the kind with the chocolate and vanilla swirled together. He still put sprinkles on the top. Tommy had always liked his sprinkles.

"So I'm thinking," Tommy said, eating his ice cream, "that I might try school again next year, after I have some money saved up. Like, maybe vocational school. But the tattooing thing could also still work out. Did I show you—"

He unbuttoned his shirt cuff and rolled up the sleeve on the left side, revealing his forearm. There was a Celtic cross tattooed on the inside in black, not badly drawn, a little wobbly where it crossed a tendon. The skin around the design was blotchy and hot-looking, and tiny red dots made a trail across the length of his arm, all the way up to the bend in his elbow.

"Mikey let me use his gun, and I hear the guy at the Purple Dragon in Bowling Green is looking for an apprentice. That's good money. I mean, that would be awesome …"

Jacob stopped hearing him. He watched Tommy's mouth—the lips so much like his mother's—forming words, empty things Nora would never have said, or believed. He wondered about Helen, whom he'd last seen on Christmas Eve, by accident. This was at Wal-Mart. She was standing over by a display in the holiday aisle—a big table with a Christmas village built on it, fiber-fill snow and ceramic houses lit from within by tiny bulbs, miniature cedar trees, a train. The train circled the village, making an electronic whistle every time it rounded a corner. Helen watched the train. Jacob watched Helen. She never saw him.

Elevator
Thom Ward

He couldn't wait for his successes so he went on without them.
It seemed an adequate strategy as time and space are involved
in our consciousness, not abstractions outside the mind. He
favored the absurdity of addressing each day's tasks to the
absurdity of ignoring such work. And who could project what
might show up, the action of the mind itself unpredictable. He
washed clothes, cut grass, scrubbed the bathroom floor. All the
while he felt as if he should advance something else, a particular
competence beyond his trajectory of chores. If he played alto sax,
rode a unicycle or spoke Chinese, his talent would offer a
substantial heft and shape. People might know him by it, and,
perhaps, he could stop moving in his mind so furiously. Of course,
this particular competence would advance its own rhythm, involve
patience and discipline, and, most certainly, sacrifice. He wasn't
sure if he was ready for that, though he cringed at the thought of
being known by his trajectory of chores, one absurdity instead of
another. He couldn't wait for his successes so he went on without
them. And while he slept he was a man whose face was on the
pillow but whose eyes were on the elevator, each door exposing
and concealing that distinctive gift still unknown to him.

Only Insomnia
Gaylord Brewer

You stand before the unpolished bar
of the bodega with what spare dignity
one may muster for these hours.
What is the time? It is late, friend.
You stand, quietly alone in the residue

of a smile for a prayer of nothing.
You still see the old man, deaf
but nearly steady, departing the café,
vanquished to night and perhaps
a bed, perhaps a dreamless sleep.

You hope so. Other possibilities,
they are less good. And your confident
young friend, with humbling lessons
to learn—but not tonight, not tonight—
he is most certainly home, woman

soft against the angular certainties
of his body. Now you too, friend,
must leave, turn from the barman
who has turned from you, step cautiously
from these oblique and pleasant lights

and again toward the late shadows
of the trees. So late, in fact, it will
soon be early once more. How strange.
With dawn, perhaps you too shall
sleep, and that is all you ask of mercy.

Burning
Gaylord Brewer

A father accused, a son, a smell of cheese.
The boy on a keg of nails, his feral gut twisted
with wanting. The Justice cracks the hammer,
case dismissed and they're back on the wagon,
the whole ragged family, the busted stove,
the silent clock pointing the way clear of town.

You study this wretched cycle, find yourself
when the father strikes you, his black immensity
carved in light of stingy fire, your second
beating of the day. He's wrong: *You'd have lied
for him, you'd have done it.* Twenty years
passed, you still taste that Snopes blood fierce

on your tongue, still hear the gunshots,
still walk a dream of black trees all around.
Twenty years and waking to the agonized truth,
your heart's pull and despair, waking cold
with the old man's limp. Whippoorwills still
predict the dawn as you walk the stiffness away.

Civilians

Brian Weinberg

IT WAS PAST midnight when Wayne and I got into the back seat of his mother's station wagon. We'd been in the basement, watching an action movie with Wayne's father, when Wayne asked if we could go for a ride. Mr. Kitchens exhaled cigarette smoke and said, "Your mother locked in?" Wayne went upstairs to check. A ride sounded like a good idea to me—I hoped we could go in Mr. Kitchens' unmarked car, but was too shy to ask. He kept his eyes on the TV, reclined in his La-Z-Boy, shiny brown ankle boots propped on the footrest. I could see his revolver strapped into an ankle holster.

Wayne reported she'd locked the door and the television wasn't flickering under the crack. Mr. Kitchens snorted, shook ice around in his tumbler, then cranked his chair forward. This was my third time sleeping over at Wayne's—we'd met at the neighborhood pool—and all three nights his mom had slept in the spare room. I was ten years old, like Wayne, and didn't give much thought to Wayne's parents sleeping separately, except to think that it was weird. Mornings, after Mr. Kitchens left for work, I liked peeking into the master bedroom. I wanted to see how messy Mr. Kitchens could be, his civilian clothes strewn on the floor.

~~~

Wayne might have sat up front, but the passenger seat was occupied by his mother's CPR mannequin, a guy with messy black hair, wearing his seat belt. I thought it was funny she drove around that way. Mr. Kitchens and Wayne didn't seem to notice.

As we cruised the quiet subdivision, Wayne shined a long black flashlight, an alloy police issue, onto the back of Mr. Kitchens' head. Mr. Kitchens changed the angle of the rearview mirror without saying anything. His neck was razor burned and crosshatched with creases. He drove slowly, stroking his cheek, easing through turns.

Wayne started giggling. Mr. Kitchens tossed his hands into the air and said, "I'm busted." I put my hand over my mouth—it was more exciting than funny. I didn't know how much flashlight Mr. Kitchens would tolerate. And my own father, a professor, didn't say words like "busted," didn't take me for drives late at night. It occured to me that driving at night with lights inside the car wasn't safe. I knew this because my father had criticized my mother for using the dome light. My parents hardly ever argued, but sometimes they criticized. No way was I going to criticize Mr. Kitchens or Wayne. We were having a good time.

Mr. Kitchens pushed in the dash lighter. Wayne turned the flashlight into my eyes. I blocked the beam and said, "Quit it," but he waggled the light instead. I looked out my window: through the strobing glare, the houses looked haunted.

Mr. Kitchens patted the mannequin hard on its head. "Your mother's new boyfriend," he said, then lit his cigarette. I hoped he hadn't noticed Wayne treating me like a punk. In the reflection of my window, Wayne had put his mouth around the end of the flashlight, so his cheeks glowed red. He tapped my shoulder, but I wouldn't turn around. He grunted a few times, and still I wouldn't look. I imagined his winged shoulder blades, his skeletal chest. It wasn't the first time I had sized him up.

At the pool, Wayne was famous for his intentional belly-flops off the high dive, which caused the lifeguards to blow their whistles. At home, he had great toys, a bottomless tin of candy on the kitchen counter, and no brothers or sisters to harass us. But the first time I slept over, he pretended to accidentally slice his hand with his army issue survival knife. He rolled around on his bedroom floor, holding his hand to his chest and moaning, until I got scared.

"Should I get your mom?" I asked.

"Yeah, get my mom," he said.

She was in the kitchen, kneeling over the mannequin and talking to an imaginary class. Her long blonde hair was pinned up in heaps. She said, "Okay, any questions on checking the carotid pulse?"

"Wayne needs you," I said.

She looked over her shoulder and said, "What for?"

"He cut his hand," I said.

By the time we got back to his room, he was crying actual tears. His mother just stood in the doorway, hands on hips. She said, "If you're fak-ing…" Wayne shook his head No. His mother began rolling her CPR manual into a club, moving slowly toward Wayne. When she started to squat down, Wayne popped to his feet and made for the door. "Dip shits!" he shouted. His mother chased him with the manual, the skin under her arm flapping as she whacked. "Rat! Rat! Rat!" she shouted, and Wayne shouted, "Take cover!" as he galloped down the basement steps.

"Jim, he's out of control!" she shouted down the steps. I couldn't have agreed more and wanted to get even, but after standing in his room for a while, couldn't think of anything to do besides go downstairs.

Down in the paneled basement, Mr. Kitchens was watching a cop movie and didn't seem angry at Wayne. He spoke only once in what must have been an hour, pointing at the television, shaking his head as he explained how in real life, a patrolman would call in an 11-99, officer needs help. A few minutes later, he said, "Officer needs help," and went to the store.

"I'm bored," I told Wayne. "Cops flying hang gliders is corny."

"My dad has *Playboys*," he said.

"Get 'em!" I said.

Wayne went upstairs and returned with three *Playboys*. I flipped through two before Mr. Kitchens came home, and we had to shove them under the couch. It seemed like Mr. Kitchens was in a great mood. He'd picked up lottery tickets for Wayne and me, and I won twenty dollars, and later, he demonstrated pressure points, so Wayne and I could use them on bullies. He pressed into a sensitive spot under my jaw, but I didn't pull away. "Hey, you got a high tolerance for pain," he told me. I went home the next afternoon thinking Mr. Kitchens was cool.

~~~

Wayne switched off the flashlight just as his father switched off the headlights. We were pulling over to the curb in an undeveloped part of the subdivision. I sat forward, curious about what was going on. Mr. Kitchens put the car in park. Wayne said, "Pinball," and sounded excited. Mr. Kitchens got out, leaving his door open, the engine running. He walked to the middle of the street, looking up at the sky. He was short and muscular, with arms as big as bazookas. He stooped over and went into his boot. He stood up holding a flask.

"What are we doing?" I asked, but Wayne was already getting out. I hopped out also, and stood on the tree lawn. "We have to put the back seat down," said Wayne, coming around to my side. Mr. Kitchens and Wayne leaned into opposite doors, unhooked latches, and together, collapsed the seat back. The rear of the station wagon was one smooth sheet of steel. Wayne backed away and held out his hand to invite me inside. I stepped forward then hesitated. "What's going on?" I asked. Wayne shoved me from behind. "Go on," he said. "It's fun."

I sat kneeling with my head pressed into the foam roof. Mr. Kitchens was still looking in through the door. Moonlight, or maybe a streetlight, allowed our eyes to meet. His were all pupil. They tested me as they might test a suspect. I turned my head away. "You're not a pussy, are you?" he asked. I shook my head No. "Wayne tell you not to tell your parents?" he asked. Wayne hadn't told me a thing, but I nodded. "Okay," Mr. Kitchens said, and shut the door.

Wayne and I lay side by side on our stomachs, facing the front of the car. My heart was pounding into the cool metal. Mr. Kitchens switched on the headlights, shifted the car into drive, and glanced over his shoulder.

"Ready?" he asked. "Ready," Wayne said. "Blast-off," said Mr. Kitchens, and floored the accelerator. Wayne and I slid backwards, our heads knocking together, our shoes thudding on the tailgate. Mr. Kitchens hit the brakes, launching us headfirst into the front seat. My cheek jammed into my shoulder and my neck made a popping sound. Mr. Kitchens didn't stop screeching the tires and Wayne's arms and legs tangled with mine, sliding back again, forward again, and then it all stopped and Mr. Kitchens turned around.

"Dead yet?" he asked.

"No way," said Wayne.

I couldn't breathe, couldn't think. Mr. Kitchens unbuckled the mannequin and passed it over the seat to Wayne. "Arthur wants to join you," he said, and both he and Wayne laughed. Then Mr. Kitchens squealed the tires again, jerking the wheel left and right, so Wayne and I rolled into the hard sides of the cargo area, the wheel wells. We tumbled over each other, bone cracking on bone, the mannequin's heavy rubber limbs smacking into us. Wayne's tooth gouged my scalp, and it didn't seem like Mr. Kitchens was going to stop until we were dead. I closed my eyes, expecting to die. Soon, a numbness came over me. I was tumbling through outer space. I saw my parents at my funeral, crying their heads off. I listened to Wayne's hiccupy breaths, his groans as he smashed into the tailgate, the seat back. I wanted to scream.

~~~

Wayne lay face up with his arms out, blinking, his chest rising and falling. Mr. Kitchens looked over his shoulder. I sat up and held my hand to my head. My hair was sticky with blood. "I'm bleeding," I said. Mr. Kitchens was looking at my hand against my head, but didn't say anything. "I'm bleeding!" I shouted. Mr. Kitchens' head snapped around. Wayne sat up and looked at me angrily. Mr. Kitchens pushed in the dash lighter. The mannequin was upside down against the rear window, its arms and legs bent at crazy angles.

~~~

He took me into the bathroom off the master bedroom. He put the toilet seat down and pointed. He'd told Wayne to get lost. I sat there. He opened the medicine cabinet and rummaged for supplies. It felt like the bleeding had stopped. On the sink he arrayed cotton balls, a bottle of rubbing alcohol, a box of Band-Aids. He removed his wedding band, setting it on the sink with a sharp click. He washed his hands with a green bar of soap.

He began blotting alcohol onto my head.

"Geez," I said. The wound was stinging, my head was bouncing around.

"You have the right to remain silent and refuse to answer questions," he said. "Do you understand?"

"You're gonna make it start bleeding again," I said.

"Do you understand?" he asked.

I nodded.

"Anything you do say may be used in the court of law. Do you understand?"

I nodded again. He gave a soft chuckle. I decided not to be Wayne's friend anymore. I said, "Stop it," and put my hand over the cut.

He removed my hand, and started blotting again. "I know First Aid," he said.

I hated the sound of his voice.

"Now *there's* something we can agree on," he said. "How to properly dress a wound. My wife teaches First Aid, you know that? Well, she's learning to teach it. If she gets certified, which she probably will, she may quit triage and be a full-time teacher. She likes teaching because it's a big change, but I'm wondering if that's a good enough reason to like something. Know what I mean?"

I stood up. I was going to cry, but told myself to wait. I wanted to go home. He was standing between me and the door. I kept my eyes on the floor.

"You pissed off?" he asked.

I nodded.

"We've never done it with another person," he said.

"So?" I said.

"So my son thinks it's fun," he said.

"Not really," I said.

"Nobody ever got hurt before," he said.

"Well I'm hurt now," I said.

"You going to tell your parents?" he asked.

"No," I answered.

"Good man," he said, and let me go.

Outside Fason's Butcher Shop The Sign Proclaims Nostalgia Racers For Christ

Rick Campbell

When I tell my daughter about the wounds,
I say Roman soldiers with long
pointed spears jabbed him
when he was on the cross. I pick
Roman soldiers because essentially
Romans could represent nostalgia,
especially to a five-year-old
in the year 2000, and soldiers
no matter who or where or when
can be believed to jab someone

with spears. It's the nature
of their mission. I skip the part
of the story with the nails
in the palms. I skip the part
about being God—Mary's son,
that's enough. Mary the Great Mother
who in our house sees and protects
and brings babies to those who wait
ten long years on earth.

Now as I pass the sign
I wonder if these are old stock cars
roaring around a dirt track—Tbird,
Charger, Cougar, Chevelle
396—out somewhere
in the paper mill pines,
and if these are old motorheads
driving old muscle cars,
remembering an old time religion
of slamming through gears
and slick wide tires.

If their Christ was better then,
if it's the Christ of the Firebird
mourning the coming of Camrys,
minivans and SUVs,
if one needs the Cobra Jet 429,
the 396, the Hemi , roaring
glasspacks and a Hurst on the floor,
fast cars giving themselves to Jesus.

Each day I see this sign
and think of racing cars
and the haunches of pigs,
the ribs of cows, thick-cut bacon,
sausage, of entrails washed
out to slop, of blood dripping
to the sand.

The Body As Instrument
Rick Campbell

The body can be an instrument
of measure. You stand with legs spread
firm on the earth, and stretch your arms
out to your sides, true and straight. You sight
down each arm, your body forming the 180 degree line,
and then you bring your arms together in front of your nose,
sight that line to the next horizon,
and there's the right angle you walk.
Why? Maybe you're looking for something.
Maybe plotting or plodding the boundary
of a field, or more boring, the corner
of a lot that will be like the lot like the lot
like the lot next to it. And white 3-bedroom
houses will sprout here. And palm trees
will be set here, propped up by sticks. You
walk your line; each measured time your right
foot hits the earth you add 5—a counting
rhyme in your head—5,10, 15, 20.
You try not to vary your stride—25, 30
35, 40—because if every right foot hits true
the point you are looking for will be near
what your pacing's supposed to yield. We
took pride in measuring distance with our feet,
turning angles by hand, eyeballing plumb
without a range rod and level. Our bodies
were an act of love, a certainty more than machine.
We wanted to find our reference points, traverse
our way across field or swamp, subdivision
or highway curve, without the theodolite's
turned angles. Let us walk we said,
let us lay our bodies down.

Monster Hits
Mick Cochrane

WILSON'S PRESCHOOL TEACHER called around ten o'clock to say that he was upset, beyond upset, he was curled up in the block area, sobbing. It took awhile, but finally, she'd pulled it out of him, what was the matter. He believed that when he got home that afternoon, she was going to be bald.

Martha had explained it to him the night before. After book stories and before she rubbed his feet. She'd used the phrase "powerful medicine," something she'd read in a pamphlet, stupidly repeated it again and again until it dissolved into utter nonsense. Pofolmedsin. (She really thought of it as poison, but no matter.)

"So you're gonna be bald," he said. It wasn't a question; it was an accusation.

"Well, yes," she'd said. He turned to the wall then. "But just for a little while," she said.

"You can leave now," he said. "Good night."

~~~

She'd planned to give Ellis a more detailed account, throw in a little biochemistry maybe, make it a Learning Experience even. His third grade class was studying Life Science, the food chain and photosynthesis. He was a kid who'd woken her up once at 5 in the morning—he was five at the time—by suggesting, "Mommy, let's talk about molecules," an incessantly, sometimes exhaustingly, curious child. But he'd cut her off almost immediately. Held a waggling hand in the air, like a palsied traffic cop. "But then," he said. "You'll be cancer-free." It was a gesture he'd always used to hold the world at bay, to pause while he found the silver-lining, the glass half-full, some sliver of hope or consolation in the face of what was disturbing or disruptive, whether it was a villain ("But he wants to be good, right?") or a neighbor's dead cat ("she was tired, she needed a long rest, don't you think?").

"Yes," she'd told him.

"You *are* cancer-free now, right?" he said. She wondered where he'd picked up that locution, cancer-free, it wasn't something she'd ever said. Other kids brought obscenities home from school, exotic swear words, but hers picked up medical jargon.

Ellis understood very well what the surgery had been about. But there was something, maybe something, in the latest scan, a murky spot. It was what she imagined late at night, the house quiet, Fred breathing heavily beside her, and inside her, something malign and multiplying. She could almost hear it, a vicious, busy whir.

She didn't like to lie. She let Fred field all inquiries regarding Santa Claus. "Well," she said.

"You're *practically* cancer-free now, right?" Ellis said.

"Practically," she said.

~~~

Wilson was waiting in the office for her, jacketed, booted, flap-hat on his head, backpack at his feet. He looked forlorn, a sad little man about to board a Greyhound bound for some uncertain future. She smiled at the receptionist, in her best, new, cheerful, not-dead-yet fashion and signed him out.

She got him buckled into the back seat and put the car in gear. It was a dismal February Minnesota day, gray skies, exhaust-encrusted mounds of snow lining the curbs. It had been a brown Christmas. The week before, the Groundhog had seen his shadow, which meant six more weeks of winter, but Martha could never remember whether that was good or bad. Wilson let out a convulsive, sobbing breath and stared out the window. To hell with the pamphlets, she decided, all that cautious, touchy-feely crap. You have to be definite. No waffling, no dithering, no shilly-shallying. Take charge.

"Listen up," she said. It was what her high school basketball coach used to say during timeouts. Then she would tell them what was going to happen—a pick, a pass, and score—drew it on her clipboard with red grease pencil, a little narrative of success. There was no "if" or "maybe" in Coach Connell's vocabulary. She spoke in muscular declarative sentences and didn't take questions.

Martha caught Wilson's eye in the mirror. Suddenly, on this new frequency, she had his attention. He was all ears. She didn't know exactly what she was going to say, but she plowed ahead anyway.

"You don't have to worry," she said. "There's absolutely nothing to worry about. You know why? I'll tell you why. Because I'm going to get—"

Wilson's eyes seem to widen. What? What was she going to get?

"I'm going to get replacement hair," she said. "I've made arrangements. Done and done. Problem solved. So you have nothing to worry about, Mr. Wilson. Nothing at all. I've got things under control."

When she was still in junior high school, she used to baby-sit for the Petersons, a family across the street. They had two little girls and a sweet-tempered, slightly arthritic chocolate lab named Brutus. She loved his calm, brown presence in the house, the fact that always and everywhere, he was happy to see her. She had zits then, a mouth full of metal, and a flat chest, but Brutus didn't care. She could leave the room, return five minutes later, and thump, thump, thump, his tail on the floor would signal his pleasure in her presence. But the dog was terrified of thunder storms—would howl and whimper, hide in the basement, shake and even shed with fear. If there was a storm, Mr. Peterson instructed her, she was to look Brutus in the eye and tell him firmly, "There's nothing to worry about, Brutus. I've got things under control."

Once, one summer night, a storm did blow in. There was a flash of lightening in the distance, some rumblings overhead. She made her little set speech to the dog. Spoke with as much conviction as she could muster. *There's nothing to worry about. I've got things under control.* Kept a straight face. But it was funny to hear herself so matter-of-factly claiming such power. Beyond that, there was something heartbreaking and pure about Brutus, his big-headed, brown-eyed trust—in her, a fourteen-year-old gum-chewing god, his absolute faith in her absurd claim.

~~~

That night, after dinner, she told Fred about it, how instantly mollified Wilson had been.

"Replacement hair?"

"I didn't want to say 'wig,'" she said. "It sounds so, I don't know, so fake, so desperate."

She'd already come to despise the lexicon of illness, this new vocabulary being forced upon her. Words she didn't want in her mouth.

She used to think a port was a city with a harbor for ships. Used to be, a port was New York, a port was Boston. Now it was spigot in her neck, like the tap in a beer keg, where they drew the blood and poured in her medicine.

She disliked the word "survivor" but there was no other term for it, what she aspired to. There wasn't much nuance, not a lot of room for nice distinctions. There were survivors, and there were the rest, non-survivors, un-survivors, otherwise known as dead people. "So what's the prognosis?" she had been asked again and again, not unkindly, a question that meant, as far as she could tell, what—expressed in mathematically precise terms—are the chances that in say, five years, you'll be alive? As if they were making book on her in Vegas. What does Jimmy the Greek say? What are the existential odds? What's the point spread in the Cancer Bowl? Sometimes she lied; sometimes she changed the subject. She imagined getting all crazy-rude, doing a little DeNiro—"Am I going to die? Is that what you're asking? Why would you ask me that? You got a lotta nerve"—but she knew it wouldn't help to bully some poor, nervous, well-meaning soul. Still, she was tempted.

Illness had not made her heroic, not even, as far as she could tell, an ever-so-slightly better person, not yet anyway. Maybe that came later. She was receptive to it, willing even to be transformed. But for now, she felt like the same deeply flawed person she'd always been, still capable of indolence and impatience. If anything, she feared, she detected a new mean streak. For one thing, she was harboring some terrible private thoughts. Believing not just that she did not deserve cancer, but thinking of those who should have it instead, or at least first—let them go ahead while she lingered for a few more years at the back of the line. Women, for example, whose children were already grown, or at least older, within striking distance of graduation anyway. Best candidates of all, unpleasant, miserable people with no children. She was prepared to point out individuals, to name names. The biddy across the street. The bitch ahead of her at a traffic signal in her Volvo on a cell phone. Her sister-in-law Alice, who was a hypochondriac and some kind of medical procedure junkie—sampling Urgent Care facilities around town like new restaurants, settling in on the couch at night with a bowl of popcorn to watch the Health Channel, who seemed to flush with something like sexual excitement while she discussed one of her recent probes or scans. Why not her? She seemed like a perfect candidate for a serious illness.

~~~

One of the Monday morning girls—she thought of them as the Chemo Klatch—called it Retail Therapy. Women would suffer through their chemo, radiation, whatever experimental torture the doctors had cooked up—and then go out and buy Big Stuff. Clothes, jewelry, major appliances. Drag in the bags, too queasy to unpack them. Knowing that after years of furtive shopping, nobody, but nobody, not even the tightest, budget cop of a husband, was even going to ask. It was carte blanche, the make-a-wish effect. There were legends. One woman with Stage 4 ovarian cancer, given a one percent shot by her Mayo doctors, in the midst of killer chemo—six hours a pop, an eight-month run—bought a boat. On impulse. Turned into the showroom on the way home from the hospital and signed the papers. Never been on the water before, but so what, the thought of it, the cool feel of fiberglass under her fingers, calmed her down, made her feel less toxic. (And now, five years later—this is the legend, what a friend of a friend knows for a fact—she's on Minnetonka every weekend, tan and strong, a regular sailin' babe, laughing at the geniuses in Rochester.)

It didn't sound like the sort of thing she would go in for. For her shopping was a necessity, not root canal, but definitely not mood altering either. If she needed something, she bought it. Same with Fred. She didn't go to the mall for recreation. If she wanted to be entertained, she went to the movies.

But there she was Friday morning in the Schmitt Music showroom in Southdale trying out keyboards.

The day before, at her treatment, she got talking to her nurse about music. This woman was in a band, played guitar and wrote songs. They'd just made a CD. She didn't say so exactly, but there was something about this woman's manner—her name was Solvig, blonde, blue-eyed, skin like a Noxzema model, she was a Norwegian angel—that made Martha suspect her music, if not downright Christian, was decidedly upbeat. Before, she might have laughed at the idea of inspirational music, Cancer Rock.

"What about you?" Solvig wanted to know. "Do you play?"

"Used to."

When it was time to begin, Solvig had said quietly, "Starting at 9:07." Martha started to cry, then, just a little—that somber announcement made it suddenly real—and she touched her shoulder.

"Used to," Solvig had said. "I don't like the sound of that. Why used to?"

As a little girl, Martha had taken lessons, Wednesday afternoons with Mrs. Moser, who had a German accent, whose house smelled liked cinnamon and warm dough, an apple pie factory.

At home, Martha practiced lazily on the family's scarred upright. She dutifully learned and performed her recital pieces. What she most enjoyed was picking out top-forty tunes by ear, making up her own Joni Mitchell melodies and singing quietly to herself, her own lyrics—mostly tortured, lower case notebook poetry, miserable stuff, no doubt, that oddly cheered her. Those songs were her secret, inner life, a diary no one would ever pry into.

Later, when she was in college, she did some time in a wedding band. Playing "Proud Mary" and the Beer Barrel Polka for happy drunks. She liked the camaraderie; and even though she was painfully self-conscious herself, she loved to see other people dancing, all that sweating and grinning. Then their bass player and spiritual leader—he owned all the amps and had a station wagon—got a gig in a Van Morrison tribute band, and that was the end of it.

Why 'used to'? "Who knows why," Martha said. "Life is full of used to's."
When they'd moved her mother out of the house into an apartment, she'd
given the piano away. Martha was studying for the bar at the time, spending ten hours a day in the library, lugging those loathsome review books
around, living on coffee and vending machine snacks. A most unmusical
life. A little bit of herself left behind at some point. No big deal. That's
what you tell yourself.

When Solvig had unhooked her, Martha felt like she should say something. "What doesn't kill me makes me stronger," she said. "Right?" It was
one of her brother Joe's trademark lines, what he used to say when he was
shit-faced, reeling from his own favorite powerful medicine. She missed
him. Now he was a sober, gray-haired stranger, living in Alaska. He sent
her encouraging emails and digital photographs of himself and his second
wife and their crazed-looking bulldog named Ethel.

Solvig patted her arm. She didn't seem too impressed by brave and clever
bullshit. "You should get an instrument," she said. "You need some music."

A young salesman—Vince, his name tag read—followed her around,
peppering her with too much information, all about tone layers and
auto-accompaniments and programmable rhythm patterns. He had hair
highlighted a color she associated with artificial suntans, an earring, a boxy
three-button suit coat that made him look like a hip Western lawman,
Wyatt Earp with an attitude.

She sat down and rested her fingers on a keyboard. Played a couple of
cautious chords with her left hand. Somehow her hands remembered. It
was a floor model, marked down. She felt a rupture in her chest, deeper,
more fundamental than a sob, an earthquake of grief she would not permit,
not here, not now.

Vince the boy salesman launched into a spiel about no interest payment
plans, but she cut him off.

"I'll take it," she said.

Vince started to write it up quick, before she changed her mind. He
threw in a pile of song books. They made a little small talk—the weather,
traffic on 494, the new lights on the on-ramps—and he admitted that he
was new on the job.

"You'd never know it," she told him. "You seem like an old pro. A sea-
soned sales professional."

"Really?" he said.

"Absolutely," she said.

Before long, she knew all about Vince. He had a fiancé named Tammy.
He even produced a picture from his wallet. The deal was done, they were

finished with business, but Vince kept talking, telling her all about his big plans, how he was living with his parents now but saving for a house while Tammy worked for her associate's degree at Normandale.

He was maybe twenty years old, Martha figured. A baby. She had just turned forty, she was old enough to be his mother.

He was a nice boy; she wished him well. She wished his fiancé well, too. Tammy. A long and happy life together. If he asked, she'd play at their wedding. She wished them two kids and a house full of laughter. And no cancer.

~~~

At home, it sat splay-footed in the dining room, like an ironing board. By the time Fred got home with the boys, she'd worked her way through most of Monster Hits of the 70s. "Crocodile Rock." "You're So Vain." "Hotel California." "Let It Be." "Fire and Rain."

Fred didn't bat an eye. You'd think she bought pianos all the time. Another day, another instrument. "Cool," is what he said.

She serenaded him while he moved around in the kitchen putting dinner together. The absolute very best thing about cancer was the food. Ever since her diagnosis, they'd been eating like kings. Neighbors, people from her firm, from Fred's school, it seemed like everybody brought something. Lasagnas, pasta salads, whole roasted chickens, vats of soup, crock-pots full of stew, long loaves of French bread. One day Martha looked out the window and there was a woman she'd never seen before, a complete stranger—she wore owlish round glasses, a lumpy overcoat, and a big plaid tam-o'-shanter, she didn't even look like the *sort* of person they would know—leaving a cardboard flat full of food on their welcome mat.

It was a steady stream of food, something almost every day, and it had not let up. Their refrigerator was stuffed. A pot roast. Quiches. Takeout from Broder's pasta and Rudolph's barbeque. Two Poppin' Fresh pies. It was overkill—her appetite came and went, Wilson ate practically nothing but peanut butter and chicken nuggets—but all that food gave her a sense of well being. Every night was a church picnic, a homely pot luck. Casseroles with masking tapes names on the bottom, index cards with handwritten instructions—they made her feel loved.

Martha could tell when Fred was heating things up and setting out dishes, lining up the bottles of salad dressing, that he thought he was cooking. He wasn't literally wearing an apron, but he assumed that sort of cheerful, pink-cheeked, flour-dusted busyness. He made a happy commotion in the kitchen, and she was glad that he could feel useful. She fiddled with the settings, shifted into organ mode, and played some hockey-style fills to cheer him on. *"Let's go, Fredy-O…"*

He smiled, raised a triumphant fist in the air, and went back to grating cheese. For Wilson, she worked out a simple percussive arrangement of "If You're Happy and You Know It." He was now, it turned out, happy, and he knew it, so he clapped his hands, stomped his feet, and patted his head. For Ellis, she played the opening of the Star Wars theme.

After dinner they drank coffee and the boys busied themselves at their feet. Ellis lay on his belly, biting his lip in concentration, his new wire-rimmed glasses perched on his nose, giving him the look of a little scholar, young Woodrow Wilson, writing in a notebook.

"How do you spell 'schedule' again?" he wanted to know. Recently, having become fascinated by Fred's black leather day planner, he'd begun planning his own days, creating elaborate grids he never followed. Tomorrow was Saturday: Eight o'clock: brush teeth. Eight thirty: breakfast. After that: Clean room, read, draw, snack, and finally, the rest of the day, more generally, she was happy to see, devoted to—all caps—FUN.

Wilson was up to his elbows in his Lego bin, building an enclosure for his plastic big cats, an elaborate structure with spires and towers, some kind of Gothic zoo.

Fred talked about his day, some new state-mandated test he had to deal with, and she tugged idly at her hair, recently cut so it would perfectly match the wig—her replacement hair—that had been made for her. Life imitates art. Any day, it was supposed to happen. She had been shedding, but just a little. When it started in earnest, she'd get her head shaved. She was overdue—it was probably the shampoo the wig lady recommended, Nixoran, it was called, which sounded like something to stop smoking but actually was for people with thinning hair and was supposed to help it come back in time. She had a box full of hats, and was eager to get on with it.

"Why don't you play something?" Fred asked. He must have caught her drifting off. "Go on," he said. "Tickle the ivories."

She sat down on the bench, and Fred leaned over her, Bogey-style. "Smoke on the Water," he said.

"Oh be quiet," she said.

They both started laughing. Martha saw Ellis shoot his brother one of those what's-up-with-them looks and shrug.

She leaned into Fred and whispered. "Cancer is so much fun," she said.

Reading Kundera at 6 A.M.
Silvia Curbelo

It was the year nobody slept.
All night the world ran east
and west along that coast.
You liked living alone.
You were clinically hopeful.

Of all the windows in all
the burning cities, yours
was the one with the most
reckless view, a notion
laced with gasoline.

You were standing
on the side of the road
when I drove through,
the future waiting like
a warm piece of bread.

Imagine a decade is a river,
like water under the bridge
without the bridge. Somewhere
between the accidental blue
of the winter sky and the long ash
of your French cigarette I knew
the metaphors would fail us.
The way the end of desire
has its own gravity, the books
falling open to the wrong
pages all of our lives.

Modern Art
Silvia Curbelo

Watching you turn the pages of Pischel's
A World History of Art I think of man's
relentless gamble towards the 21st century,
somewhere between the blueprint
of the wheel and the actual, immeasurable
shape of longing, how the heart's
a wayward miracle, and who can say
what might happen as you pause
for a moment, electric
in your green and blue sweater,
so much like the sky nestled between
the accidental light and Cezanne's
flowering fields, as beautiful
as being finally alive, then mulling it
over coffee, the impossible bluff of
Western civilization, not unlike
this business of growing old together,
when suddenly the music stops
and the room holds its breath
for a while until all the air
is stacked between us
like a house of cards, astonished
as the moment you kiss me
and the whole towering mess
comes tumbling down.

Only Curving Lines

Janet McNally

THERE WAS A feeling she had, after leaving her homeland for another, that the new place wasn't quite right. Perhaps, she thought, it was something about the way the grass felt under her feet (a certain unfamiliar sponginess, or a thick hollowness under her footsteps like clay) or even the smell of the air. This feeling was mostly subconscious, something she had never noticed before—just what would it smell like right now in Russia, if she had stood with her feet planted apart on the street where they had lived and inhaled deeply? Since she emigrated it had been hard to pull up the feeling. Now, Tatiana admitted to herself, while unwrapping heavy crystal glasses from crumpled newspaper, she might never have thought of it again—it was years since they moved to the States—had she not come to this new apartment.

It was much like their first move. She had struggled to open the front door with a heavy bag slung over her shoulder, boxes at her feet. She turned the unfamiliar key over in her palm, trying to figure out which way would make the grooves fit. She had more things this time, though she'd taken less than half of what she and Andrei had acquired since they had lived in their house. It was just like coming from Russia, except this time she moved alone.

She noticed right away that the new apartment had a different smell than the house she had left; rather, a particular lack of smells. Her old house had a scent that had mingled slowly over eight years, a mixture of dark brown bread and little boys and the heavily perfumed orange lilies she brought home from the flower shop. The new apartment smelled like dust with a trace of new paint, an empty smell barely strung through the molecules of air.

When she went to bed that night, her first night in the apartment, Tatiana slid in and out of sleep. She dreamt that she had bottled the scent of her old house like perfume and then ran feverishly from room to room, spilling drops of liquid on the carpets. When she woke for good at five a.m., she sat up against the wall with her sleeping bag spread out below her, wondering if the whole thing had all gone along too far to take it back.

~~~

In the beginning, Tatiana had called Andrei *Grumpy* and smiled. He came home from work and went to his green armchair like a magnet, holding a small glass of vodka while he watched television. She'd get home and ask him to go to a play, a restaurant, the ballet, if one was touring in town, but he barely moved. What was, in the beginning, a term of endearment was run ragged by experience and after a while, she stopped smiling when she said it. She would pace, a pale tiger, from wall to wall behind him and try to think of what she should say, what she should scream at the back of his head. She didn't say much of anything, couldn't really, she only talked with her friend Raisa on the phone in the kitchen a few times a week.

"Men," Raisa said, "they don't adjust as well as women. They are used to what they are used to and when they come here and it is gone they forget how to live." Raisa was older than Tatiana, but she had come from Poland only a few years before. Her English was technically perfect but the words ran together with the cadence of Eastern Europeans, linking the beginning of one word with the end of the word before it. Raisa's husband had been a scientist in Poland. Here, he couldn't speak the language at all, and didn't try to learn.

Andrei was different. Having been a literature professor in Moscow he had learned English in his late teens, so he could read James Joyce, he said. American and British professors who visited the university laughed at this, telling him that Joyce probably wasn't the easiest way to begin, and after many conversations like this Andrei's speech became fluent as well. It was his idea to leave for America, where his brother who had recently emigrated assured him that he would be able to find work as a high school teacher until he could find a university job. Russia was just beginning its slow climb to democracy when Andrei decided he wanted to leave, and it didn't seem certain it would ever reach it. He wants instant results, immediate freedom, Tatiana tried to joke to her friends. It was half a miracle they had been allowed to emigrate in the first place, some luck in the lottery of applications for visas and green cards. Only the university job never came, and he wasn't certified to teach at the public schools, so Andrei spent his days at a tiny private high school, correcting two-page essays with a red-ink pen.

Since leaving Russia Tatiana and Andrei spoke English as much as their native language. For the children, they said, so they will learn. But their sons knew English long ago and still the parents spoke two languages, even at home, because neither, and both, seemed right. And lately it was silence that filled their mouths with its empty syllables.

Tatiana hadn't said much of anything until she came home with the key to another apartment clutched in her hand and said, *let's move*. She had herself convinced that if they could just change their surroundings, if they could get out of the suffocating walls of their house, they could start over. This, she later admitted to herself, came from her job at the flower shop, the hours surrounded by vibrant blooms, all dying in one way or another. They sold plants as well, and she had seen how well some plants did when they were moved to a new pot, whether it was larger or just lined with richer soil, and she started to believe that if she repotted her family, they would thrive.

Andrei looked at her, blank-eyed, as she knelt at his feet in front of the recliner, a bright, wide smile stretched across her face.

"This is my home. Why would I leave it?" he said, his eyes hard.

Tatiana began to feel that she had dared herself to do something that she couldn't afford to give up. She could only hold that position—any position—for a certain amount of time. There was only so long she could balance, so long she could wait.

A few hours later she packed her bags alone.

~ ~ ~

In Moscow, when she was young, Tatiana had been a dancer, one of the corps in a regional ballet outside the city. The Party leaders would position themselves in the front row while all the lights were up, sitting down as if their movements were scripted, synchronized. Their uniforms were so stiff she thought they must step out of them at night and leave them in the same shape. Tatiana watched from the wings, hiding like a shadow among picket fences and flat green trees and tissue-paper flower gardens. When she danced, she couldn't see much, just the buttons and medals glinting in the stage lights. The leaders with their unbending ways liked the ballet for its unflinching rigidity, its practiced perfection. *To them, we are really only statues that move*, Tatiana's choreographer had said. *But still, it is best that they come.* Tatiana knew only this: her country's leaders wanted what she did to be beautiful, so they could show the world and say, look how we succeed here.

From time to time one of her fellow dancers would leave Moscow, just disappear without toe shoes or family members, be completely gone in an evening. Those left behind talked of it while dressing for performances, standing as swans in half-makeup, enfolded within the icy fence of mirrors. She caught her own reflection, lips scarlet and eyes wide, cataloguing the whisperings. Paris, Vienna, New York, even, places where things were easier, freer, where the sun shone more than seven days a year.

All that considered, she couldn't imagine leaving. She was only a member of the corps, a chorus dancer who synchronized each movement with twenty others, but she loved the artifice of dance, its narrative. The hip moves like this, and then the pointed toe. A thousand stories were told that way.

~~~

Tatiana chose the smaller room as her bedroom. It had the larger closet and the light flowed in from the single window and tumbled to a halt on the opposite wall. The bedroom that she had shared with Andrei at the big house had no light for most of the day, so when she changed her clothes after work, shaking out the tiny pieces of fern caught in the cuffs of her pants, it always felt like night. Here, in the late afternoon, the square of light was pale and high on the wall and she threw a clear-edged shadow.

As for the closet itself, it was so enormous that she could have stood and twirled around in it. She realized that it might be larger than the entire living spaces of people in cramped cities like Tokyo and Bejing, and after that, always pictured sleeping Japanese men lying across her sweater shelves.

The boys came to see the apartment a week after she moved in. She still hadn't brought much from the house so hadn't yet needed their help; besides, she wasn't sure she could face them. She had bought a few things—a table, two chairs, a futon—but the apartment was still more empty than not. Most of her clothes weren't there yet, and when she opened the door Mischa was holding a few of her dresses on hangers, thrust out in front of him like an offering. Alexei carried an armful of books with the silver teapot balanced on top. He had a blanket slung over his shoulder. They stood in the hall, and she stood in the doorway, hesitating, until she had enough sense to let them in.

She wanted to tell them how she had to switch apartments, from three bedrooms to two, once she realized she was going alone. "Let's hope two is enough!" said the smiling blond girl who had given her the lease, her voice rising up so far at the end that Tatiana thought it would tumble over the punctuation. When the girl said goodbye she mispronounced her name. *Tatana*, she said, without the "I," as if it were a farewell. Tatiana didn't correct her, only backed toward the door, smiling, eyes wide. *Ta-ta*, she had wanted to say. *Bye-bye*.

She wanted to tell them this, but it came out, "It's a little drab here, so far." Alexei looked up, and she continued. "Everything beige, beige, beige."

Mischa was running his fingertips over the top of the table, over the little geometric pattern that spread across it.

"Doesn't that look something like biology?" Tatiana asked, smiling. "Diagrams of cells. Tiny circles in uneven little squares."

"An uneven square is not a square, Mother," Mischa said. He smiled, too kindly, Tatiana thought. Poor old Mother in her beige box with her little table full of cells. Tatiana breathed deep, stepped back, and put on some water for tea.

~ ~ ~

Andrei was a quiet man with a mouth pulled into a straight line, a man who worried about money and illness and car accidents. He was, Tatiana often said, a man who expected appendicitis from every small pain in the side. She said it in English, and afterward she laughed, but her stomach sometimes quaked when she heard the Russian words echoing in her head. This was what her grandmother had said, speaking of the worriers in her life, those who wouldn't calm down no matter who was in power. This was what her grandmother would have said of Andre.

They met like a fairy tale, Tatiana would say breathlessly when she told the story for years afterward. She and a group of other dancers were walking back to their rooming house when she became dizzy and ill, so she stopped to lean against a peeling fence while the girls walked on. Just before Andrei came around the corner on his way home, she fainted into the late winter mud at her feet. Like a movie, she told Mischa and Alexei when they were young, your father showed up just when I needed him. He carried her, limp-limbed, down the street to his own house, and his own mother held smelling salts under Tatiana's nose as he wiped the mud from her coat.

Not long after, they married, Tatiana in a trim blue suit with flowers in her hair. She gave up dancing when she was three months pregnant with Mischa, Mikhail was his full name, throwing up every morning in the tiny bathroom at the back of the studio. She could have gone back after he was born, she supposed, but felt as if her body had been hijacked and not quite given back. Also, she was fascinated by Mischa, his round, ruddy cheeks and his little almond eyes, the pale fuzz of hair on the top of his head. She didn't want to be away every night, unrecognizable in sequins and tulle. She wanted to be a proper mother who read fairy tales to her son, not look like someone who'd fallen out of one.

When Mischa was ten they left for America as a family of four, seven-year-old Alexei completing their little square. It was Andrei's idea, and first Tatiana protested, but then it seemed like there might be something better there. Andrei's brother assured them that there was, and helped them secure visas in the spring; they moved when summer was using its last few rations of sunlight. The new country was only an idea, a ghost, until they came and set their bags down in front of the door to their new house and felt the new way the earth felt under their feet, and smelled the smell of American air.

~ ~ ~

Slowly, Tatiana learned to live in the apartment. She decorated in small, scattered ways, hung calendars and baby pictures, bought houseplants and area rugs. She tacked up photos from magazines like she had in the big house when they first arrived: the Grand Canyon, sea turtles, city skylines at night. In the living room, she pinned up a few maps as wall hangings, maps of Moscow and her birth-country as a whole, both present-day Russia and the Soviet Union of her youth. Her father, he was one for maps. He'd pull them out, old and new, and spread them across the floor. "See, Tasha, see how things change." He laughed then. "They change on this map but are really the same, with a new name for everything."

For the first time in her life, Tatiana had long conversations with her sons on the telephone—she talked to them almost every night, at least one or the other. Together they tried out a different sort of language—the words felt different, as they echoed around in the chords and wires. It was something like when she had first come to the States. She sat at the cell-diagram table or in the middle of the dining room floor, cradling the phone between her shoulder and her ear, and pictured Mischa sitting at the kitchen table, Alexei leaning back to the arm of the couch, pictured the telephone wires stretching, all the miles in between.

~ ~ ~

In January, it was decided that Mischa would stay with her for a while. Both boys had accepted Tatiana's move as they had the trading of one country for another, with eyes a little too wide open, maybe, mouths stretched a little tightly, but accepted in any case. After a few months, Mischa told Tatiana that he saw no reason to stay with his quiet, brooding father when his mother had an extra bedroom. So he came with his clothes and his books and his CD collection, his mattress tied to the top of his car the way Tatiana's bookshelf had been a few months earlier. He carried it in with the help of his brother, who looked uncomfortable and more unsure, now, of where he belonged.

Mischa unpacked his books from their boxes in piles along the wall and hung his clothes in the closet, as Tatiana wandered past his room, stopping and then continuing on each time. Finally she leaned in the doorway, one hip against the frame.

"We can bring over your chest of drawers, if you'd like," said Tatiana, "or we can buy some of those plastic totes."

"The totes would be fine," Mischa said, and Tatiana stepped back into the hallway, wondering if he was as afraid of the permanence of this little apartment as she was.

~~~

There was only one time when Andrei came over unannounced and banged on the door. Mischa was at school, and he caught Tatiana standing with her back to the door, inches away but not leaning, and she felt his pounding shake the air behind her. "*Tatiana,*" he said, proud and authoritative, "*open this door.*" He banged again and Tatiana's feet seemed stuck to the floor, dug into the plush beige carpet. She couldn't move, she wanted to, all she had to do was turn and reach and unfasten the latch, but her fingers remained curled at her sides. She was afraid for him to see her like this, alone in a nearly empty apartment. She knew she couldn't go back, and was unable to picture Andrei living in this little ivory box.

The pounding faded to knocking, which softened further, becoming a tiny rhythmic sound like a heartbeat. When she heard Andrei's voice, muffled, say, "*Tasha,*" she sank to the floor. He could only wait so long. When she finally opened the door, the hall was empty.

~~~

When Mischa brought the girl home, Tatiana had just gotten used to having another voice in the apartment besides hers, when she talked to herself, and Sally's varied language of meows. She was trying to hang curtains in her bedroom when there were two voices, one familiar and one new, dropping and skittering from wall to wall. She heard rustling in the kitchen, the cupboards opening and ice clinking in glasses. She spread the second curtain out over her mattress and went to the kitchen. Mischa sat at the cell-table drinking juice with a girl.

"Mom, this is Sam," he said.

The girl was small-boned, American with her eyes brown and round as chestnuts. Before this, most of the girls Mischa dated were Russian immigrants like him, not rich girls from Moscow with their fur-trimmed collars and wide laughing mouths, but quiet girls, blonde with icy almond-shaped eyes, pale skin, and blue nylon parkas. Their fathers had been professors or scientists of some sort or another in Russia; in America they worked in factories assembling small, unexplainable things, medical devices or cellular phone parts.

When Mischa asked Tatiana later if it would be all right if Sam stayed with them awhile, her father was an alcoholic and it was best for her not to be at home, Tatiana wondered if this would continue, if she was destined to keep taking in lost things. But she liked the way that each new addition took away some of the silence in the apartment, and so she said yes. Sam was well mannered and chatty—*Mike,* she called Mischa, as if every name in America should be reduced to one syllable.

"One son brings a cat and the other brings a girl," she said to her friend Raisa on the phone. "I'd rather a hamster," she said, but that wasn't true; she liked that her soap and shampoo were no longer the only things to line the shower's edge. She liked the bubble bath that smelled like raspberry.

Mischa was in the habit of bringing things with him when he visited the big house, things he thought his mother needed or should have. One day Tatiana came home to find a dusty box from her old attic, half-unpacked by Mischa and Sam on the kitchen table. Stockings like spiderwebs, a gray nylon leotard, a pair of white satin toe shoes. The remains of another life, laid out like a skeleton.

"My mother was a dancer," Mischa said. "The principal dancer in her corps."

"No, just one of the chorus," said Tatiana, smiling a little, her eyes downcast. Sam held the shoe in the open palm of her left hand. It had the look of something very old that had outlived its usefulness.

"That was my last pair, I think," Tatiana said. "I hadn't worn them much." Not much, just as the end, when Andrei would come to her performances and stand in the back of the hall, and Tatiana would pretend she could see him while she danced.

"I never got to dance," Sam said. "I played soccer because my brother did." She cocked her head. Here was a girl who was raised by a man.

Tatiana looked at her. Sam stood tall and straight, her hips open and shoulders back.

"You have the body of a dancer, I think," Tatiana said. Sam smiled widely.

"Show me something!" she said.

Tatiana swept her feet into first position, toes pointing out in the carpet, and Sam did the same in her orange socks. Together, they fell straight to the floor in a grande plié, first Tatiana and then Sam, brushing their fingers close to the floor.

"Why did you stop?" asked Sam, wobbling a bit as she tried to come up straight.

"Oh," Tatiana said. "It's hard to say. Things start, and they end. Who knows why?"

Everything is the same, her father had said, *with a new name for everything*. That isn't true, not really, Tatiana thought, the definitions have changed. Her new English words cannot replace the Russian like little spelled-out understudies. Her father's maps, in all their incarnations, before and after, stretch out on the wall. She has lived here, and here, the big house and her little apartment. As she *pliéd* over and over, she remembered the perfect rhythmic motion, the comfort of learning to move one's body in this way. Why had she given it up? There was this: she could only hold that position—any position—for a certain amount of time. Things would change, they would transform. You would leave everything behind: the sunless sky, the story in a pointed toe, the creaky, bent-limbed Cyrillic alphabet.

With each swooping bend toward the floor, she watched Sam become steadier.

"No elbows," Tatiana said, "only curving lines." Same raised her arms over her head in a perfect oval and Mischa smiled from his seat.

Tatiana felt she could make her body remember the way it used to be, as if all the years between had been only an intermission. Now, the lights flashed, a warning sign, and people began to return to their seats. Tatiana closed her eyes and readied herself. All of this stretched out ahead of her like the lines on the maps: the lights along the edge of the stage, the glinting buttons in the audience, the feathers trailing off the dancers' costumes like snow. ■

Little Minster Street, Winchester

Patricia Waters

Lie in bed, a single bed made of iron, in a front room, 18th century house,
great windows on two walls, so tall that when you stand in one,
your head barely comes to the upper sash, these symmetries overlook a
    small street,
scarce two blocks long, you can see across rows of painted brick,
the glossy doors, polished knockers, still-life cats sitting on windowsills
to the towers of the cathedral from where the bells reach out to you,
you are from a foreign land where there are no bells like these
that pummel the air on Sunday all day, on Wednesday evenings for
    practice.

Lie in bed, listen to the tumble and fall of the bells,
    how they pick themselves up again
            and fling their music over you.

Eat chocolate, corner your piece of sky
till you can fall into it, this happiness you wear like a dress, wear it
until it falls apart and you can only find its original color when you cut
    open the hem,
when you rip apart the seam.

To the Spire
Patricia Waters

In the center of the village
a crossroads in the great plains of wheat
golden armies surging up to mossed gray walls
a square, a church, its spire,
the mark we walk to.
We set out in the mist of early morning,
an egg wash of sky, following the ambit
of wall, quilted fields, their hedgerows,
the spire in sight, now higher, now lower,
at first a pale blue, sometime broken, line.
As the plain begins to burn with noon,
it seems to melt and coruscate
under the sun's hammer. After noon, colors
separate, harden, a steel-blue thrust.
We approach the village,
the sudden abyss between that pointing finger
and our falling-down world, twilight and swallows,
geometry of light and shadow.
These are old griefs, my dear.

The Elvis Egg
Bill Brown

for my sister

Our mother, like all mothers,
had spent Good Friday
sweating over boiled eggs,
dipping them in dyes: yellow,
red, blue, green and purple.
Some were stenciled with zig-
zags, others with dots and frills.
I was seven and you were nine
that Saturday before Easter.
It was 1957: No one would accuse
Elvis of being more popular
than Jesus, he wouldn't stand
for it, but that day he was.
As forty kids scavenged
the park for treasures,
you emerged with your basket
filled with bright candy and
hard-boiled eggs, your prize
balanced like the top boulder
of a pyramid, the Elvis egg with
"Don't be cruel to a heart that's true"
stenciled on sky blue shell.
You sang your egg to jealous
girls who squealed, swooned,
and pretended to faint, as they
swivelled their hips like the King.
You, my big sister, were queen
for a day, while sweet Jesus waited
in the tomb for the stone to roll away.

My Father Comes to Me
Bill Brown

Homage to Mark Strand

All night Heritage Creek roared
a high pitch outside our cabin—
a tropical storm churned
Southern Appalachia.

I dreamed my father took my hand
and said, "Come with me." He led
me to the little cascade where he had
stacked a tower of creek stones
to see how high he could go
before rocks teetered
and splashed in the spray.

His hair wasn't as white as when he died
but his face bore the stress of a man
who balanced a razor inside.
His mouth still held a gentleness.
I had this thought as he took my hand
and led me to the stillness of a moving pool
where he motioned for me to lean
with him over the water, and looking
down, I could see what he meant—
though his eyes were blue and mine brown,
our mouths bore the same tenderness.

"I had to die," he said, "You couldn't save me."
"I know," I said.
"You were only sixteen." he said.
"I know," I said.

"Where have you been" I asked.
"I have been stacking creek stones."
"Where have you been?"
"I have settled in the shadows
of leaves drifting toward decay."

"In what place?
"In our old yard on Sampson Ave."
"In what place?"
"In the memories of your brothers and sister."

"What do you wear?"
"I wear the grease-stained clothes of a mechanic."
"What do you wear?"
"I wear false teeth, a pocket watch and a sailor's smile."

"Why have you come?"
"To show you the shape of our mouths."
"Why have you come?"
"To study light and shadow."

"Did you lie to us?"
"Promises were made."
"Did you lie to us?"
"Silence was my only lie."

"Where will you go?"
"I will walk the pasture with my dogs, Wags and Josephus."
"Where will you go?"
"I will sleep with old house boats on the Tennessee River."

"What will you love?"
"I will always love your mother and you children."
"What will you love?"
"I will love the rain."

"What do you balance inside?"
"Nothing, the dead balance nothing."
"What do you balance inside?"
" Look in the water," he said.

Don't Hold Back

Dianne Aprile

IT WAS A brisk Tuesday afternoon in early April at the start of Japan's legitimately legendary cherry blossom season when I left Takasago, a gritty urban suburb of Tokyo, for my long trip home. The sun, symbol of an ancient nation, soaked through the rice-paper curtains of the tatami-mat bedroom where I had slept for two weeks in the home of Toshiko and Hiro Masumura. The golden-red rays fell into puddles on the stark white linens that covered my traditional Japanese futon. I remember thinking: *don't forget this. Remember every detail.* The siren wailing in the distance. The children's voices on the street, crying out in excited syllables I couldn't understand. The squawk of crows. I closed my eyes, recording it, then walked to the entry hall and the front door.

The house was uncharacteristically spacious, not at all what my son Josh had been told to expect when he was assigned to live with the Masumuras during his junior year abroad. Here, for six months, he had occupied a private suite of sorts on the ground floor, complete with kitchenette and his own bathroom. He had been warned that living space was a luxury in Tokyo and its suburbs. And yet the abundance of room and the good fortune of privacy were minor blessings compared to the gift of friendship the Masumuras had lavishly bestowed on him, and me, for these two weeks.

Now, at the front door, Josh grabbed hold of my big, black, over-stuffed suitcase, bumping it down the five steep stairs of the Masumuras' front porch. I watched anxiously as the luggage wheels crashed against each step, twisting and pivoting in distressing directions. I stood, helpless, in the entry hall, in the middle of my final rendition of the household shoe-exchange ritual, an inescapable ceremony that, despite my occasional irritation with it, I knew, in that sayonara moment, I was already beginning to miss.

Toshiko, clutching one of those tissue packets imprinted with garish nightclub ads that young people push at you on the streets of Tokyo, watched as I quickly slipped one foot and then the other out of a pair of her one-size-fits-all house shoes and then into my own dusty street shoes that had been waiting for me since I removed them the night before. I turned to hug her: me, standing in the sunken foyer where shoes and the people wearing them are consigned; she, still in slippers, standing a few inches above, on the blond-wood planks of the raised landing of the entry way. This small but significant difference in inches made us roughly the same height, a blessing as we awkwardly embraced across the social abyss that, in Japan, segregates the soft-slippered from the rough-shod.

"Come on, the train'll be here in 10 minutes," Josh shouted in English from the street, and then repeated in a louder voice in Japanese for Toshiko. To my surprise, she, too, was now slipping into street shoes and following me to the sidewalk where she unlocked the one-speed bicycle that she chained to the house each night, climbed aboard its high seat and motioned for me to toss my backpack in her wire handlebar basket. She pedaled slowly in front of us as Josh hiked my bag over uncut curbs, dragged it across bumpy train tracks and pulled it—first with one hand, then the other—down the narrow, potted-plant-lined lanes and sidewalks of Takasago.

Would I miss these crowded streets and their ubiquitous vending machines selling everything from combs and razors to bottled water and cans of beer? I wondered. Would I wish to be back on these streets where narrow wooden houses with Buddhist altars on their porches rose up between pachinko arcades and convenience stores? I wasn't sure.

But what I surely could not have known at that moment was how much I would miss Toshiko, my son's other mother, his *okaasan*, the name given to the female head of the household.

"Your son, Josh-u, he is gentle and kind."

I would miss the way she nodded vigorously, repeating "Nehhhh, nehhhh," in conversation—a word I came to understand as a sign of agreement, of conviction, of empathy, of finality. And ah, yes, her cooking, that too I would miss.

At the station, Toshiko locked up her bike and walked inside with us, as far as the ticket turnstile. We hugged again and I saw tears in her eyes, a tissue wadded in her left hand. I was too anxious to let myself absorb the obvious: that we would probably never see each other again. I didn't cry; my eyes didn't water. Josh and I, both a bit nervous about our trip to the airport, turned to head down the stairs to the track.

But I remained aware of her watching us, dabbing the tissue at her eyes, waving slowly when we turned back one final time. Or, what I thought was one final time. We noticed her a few minutes later, as we waited, at the platform, for our train. She was outside the station, on the street, leaning with one foot on her bike pedal, the other on the sidewalk that ran beside the track. And later, after we boarded the train, I caught one last glimpse of her, still standing there, watching, waving.

This had to be *me* she was watching. Josh would be back at their home in a matter of hours, to finish his semester with them. I was the one leaving for good.

It was not until after I was home a day or two that I realized how much I missed her. It didn't make sense to me at first. How could I get so close to someone with whom I could barely communicate? Who spoke to me in English for any length of time only once, when we were naked, relaxing side by side in an otherwise deserted traditional hot-springs bath, one of the outdoor *onsen* for which Japan is renowned. How could I miss someone with whom I had to use my son as translator in any significant conversation.

The time, say, at the table, when I asked what Toshiko thought of the Bush war on terrorism.

Josh told me: "She said war is not good, or maybe that the war is going badly. I'm not sure," He shrugged, tired from too many back-and-forth translations in the course of one dinner.

Or the time when I pointed to a photograph of a woman in one of her scrapbooks, and Josh explained, after listening to her say a few words in Japanese: "That's her mother who is dead."

"Ask her how old she was when her mother died?" I said, facing Josh as I spoke, then turning to face Toshiko, as he repeated to her my question, which was prompted by curiosity since my own mother's death had come to her when I was not much older than Josh. Toshiko's answer, in Josh's words, was that the death was recent.

~~~

But why, back home, did I think of her more than anyone else I met in Japan, see her face, feel a stab of grief at the thought of not seeing her again? Hiro, her husband, was kind and gracious, too. "Don't Hold Back!' was his mantra, a reflection of his desire to have me relax, ask anything, forget etiquette, do as I wished.

At first, I decided my fixation on Toshiko was an identification issue. She was my son's surrogate mother, after all. I watched her smile at him with a kind of generosity and pride that mothers reserve for their own. I noticed something—was it the way he teased her and made her laugh in spite of herself?—that reminded me of *our* relationship.

There were other points of identification. She was dark-haired and not very tall. She rarely sat still, was always jumping up to fetch a glass from the kitchen, a newspaper from the desktop, a load of laundry to hang on the outdoor clothes line. To our mutual surprise, over dinner at an inn at Mt. Fuji, we learned that we both attended Catholic high schools run by European orders of nuns; were born the same month, one year apart; married men who were entrepreneurs, who started their own small businesses.

It was at Fuji-san, in the outer room of the inn's open-air *onsen*, that Toshiko taught me the correct way to wear a *yukata*, a casual version of the better-known *kimono*. It was evening, and we were both fresh (and flushed) from the hot-spring bath, where we had relaxed together for a good half-hour in the steamy, rock-lined pool, conversing in English which Toshiko had shown a sudden interest in practicing with me. I was now towel-dry, standing in the mirrored dressing room completely naked – the Japanese way – ready to cover myself with the traditional navy blue and white *yukata* that the inn provided for those staying the night. I had just slipped my arms through its wide sleeves when Toshiko moved in front of me and said—,in Japanese—what I knew instantly had to mean, "Let me show you."

She straightened the collar, then carefully placed the right side of the open robe against my chest, then covered it with the left side of the robe.

"Must do this way," she said. "Right first."

She smiled at me, the way a mother might smile at a child before sharing a secret.

"Left-first is for the dead," she said, still smiling but with a serious tone. "It is the way of burials."

Then she unfurled the matching sash, a cross between a tuxedo cummerbund and a karate belt, made of the same patterned fabric as the *yukata*. Slowly, Toshiko showed me how to wrap and tie the sash about my waist; then, with a flourish, she added an origami-like knot that resembled an intricately cut radish or an exotic flower bud.

She stepped back, gave me a once-over and trilled her approval. When a pucker quickly gathered at the top of my robe, where the two sides met, she demonstrated the technique for dealing with a gaping collar. She grasped the edge of her robe just below the right side of her waist and tugged it gently. *Voilá*—no more gap. I followed her lead.

She must have decided I was presentable because she took me by the hand and led me up the stairs to the inn's lobby. At the first step, she said: "Do this," as she took hold of her *yukata* just above knee level and lifted the hem to about ankle-height. "Not to trip," she said, laughing into the palm of her hand.

Hiro, and Josh were waiting for us, they too dressed in their inn-issued *yukatas*. Together, the four of us walked, two by two, to the dining room for our evening meal. I remember feeling like Josh's little sister, not his mother, as he poured me a cup of sake and patiently answered my questions about the elaborate meal set before us. I had traveled with Josh to Europe, to the Grand Canyon, to beaches and resorts and dusty camps. This was the first time I found myself deferring to his greater experience.

~~~

It became routine.

"*Ohayou*," Toshiko would sing out to me when I shuffled to the dining room table each morning. "*Ohayou*," I would bounce back. And then she was off and running, setting out more food than I usually ate in a day, all for my breakfast. Perhaps it was a special spread reserved for guests. I'm not sure. But it was a mighty meal. Miso soup, a small whole grilled fish (head and all), various pickled roots and buds and grasses, a fried egg, salad doused with a creamy sesame dressing, fresh strawberries, a bowl of white rice, noodles, tofu, toast, orange juice, tea, coffee, bottled water. As I ate, she watched, urging me to eat more, obviously satisfied when I proclaimed "*oo-eeshi*"—*delicious*! If I happened to register the slightest sign, even unintended, of a need for something more, something else, she was on her feet, asking Josh to ask me what I needed, already headed for the kitchen to get whatever it was.

~~~

Later, when I was back home I found myself missing Toshiko in a quiet but melancholy kind of way. The way I sometimes thought of a dear friend who died of cancer way too young, or of my father who went out with a bang, a massive stroke taking him (and me) by surprise. But they are dead, and Toshiko lives.

"So why?" I asked my husband. "She wasn't a close friend. She wasn't my father or my …." Then I heard it, in the catch in my own voice: for a few days in April, 2005, in a suburb of Tokyo, Toshiko Masumura had been my mother. She had fed me, fussed over me, bathed with me, taught me how to dress and even speak, and then had proudly presented me, tied up in a bow, to the world.

And I had lapped it up, unconsciously but greedily. My own mother dead for so many years, years before Josh was even born, I had recognized in Toshiko (and cleaved to) the maternal intimations I had gone without, as all motherless daughters learn to do—by necessity, not intention. The small comforts, once taken for granted, now all but forgotten.

Leaving her at the train station, I must have understood, deep in my bones, as my mother used to say, that the odds were good we'd not see each other again. I didn't speak it out loud, didn't consciously record the intuition. But back home, that tender lump of awareness metastasized, forcing me to reckon with its all too familiar presence.

~~~

But oh how comfortable it had been in Toshiko's home: the downy futon she prepared for me in the room with rice-paper shades, the snow-white quilts and lace coverlets and soft-as-silk sheets; the hot baths she drew for me and the socks she insisted on washing and hanging to dry on her porch; the gifts she bestowed for no reason at all—a woodblock print from a town we visited, a cascade of hand-made characters like the ones I saw dangling from porches and posted in windows throughout Japan, a box of chocolates ("Americans love chocolate, neh?").

And of course, my goodbye gift. A *yukata*. A lovely, soft, cotton robe like the ones we wore at Fuji-san. Pale blue with swirls of petal-pink blossoms—and a belt much simpler than the one she'd tied so ornately for me. This one was better-suited for a beginner. A child, perhaps.

As I folded the *yukata* into a neat square and slipped it into my suitcase that day, Toshiko leaned her face toward mine and whispered: "Don't forget, *Right First*."

I wanted, in that moment, to hold her face with the palms of my hands, steady and close, and assure her, eye to eye, that I would never forget that it is, of course, always, inexorably, the dead who are left first.

Fevered Cold
Malcolm Glass

My head buried under thick
terry cloth, I breathed in
mentholatum steam. In the light
suffused by the towel
across the back of my head,
islands of quivering oil
drifted in the hot water.
I sat on a stool, hunched
over the basin, my face hot
in camphor mist, wheezing
a loosened rattle in my chest.
On my shoulders my mother's
hands rested, almost weightless;
and then they began their careful
ritual, kneading my fevered
muscles, her thumbs working
down between my shoulder
blades, as if searching
for hidden buds of wings.

Reveries
Malcolm Glass

I.

The curtains shape
the wind, and mold
my face, my hair
in the dancing water
of firelight.
    I lie sleeping
under the clacking
and whir of crickets,
the fine fabric of heat
pressing my arms
to the cot.
    The screens,
torn, broken, rusted,
waver like shards
of broken glass. The haze
of bees slides from bloom
to blossom beyond the sill;
and beyond the bees
the garden swims
away, ragged with
hedges, unkempt
and skeletal. The crushed
branches of hydrangeas,
long withered, nod, free
of their blue, pink
burdens.

Malcolm Glass

II.

In the copse outside
the fence, a tall
man sleeps in his taller
hat while stolid horses,
pacing the thick carpet
of violets and vinca,
stare toward the bare
fir trees on the bank
of the still pond.

I dip my paddle
in the tea-brown water
stirring small eddies
against the green boat.

A musty blue horizon
of mountains, range
after range, dies
into the skein of gray
and pale clouds muting
the sun. Amber
light falls slightly
on the firs, and shadows
begin their sly journey,
pulling fallen needles
and cones to the far side
of the moon.

Sunday Morning, Small Mercy

Brian Barker

The ramshackle cul-de-sac's
in full leaf at last, and the bright redbud
blossoms soften the slumping
houses, clusters of trumpet vine
and honeysuckle banking the bend
where daily the train rattles past.
Ubiquitous birdsong,
and last night's rain transformed
the potholes into iridescent lagoons
where starlings skirl and preen.
This morning the neighbor's calico
watched two birds build a nest
in a rust-pitted satellite dish,
and now she swaggers
home, jaws bulging, plopping down
on a sunshot patch of gravel.
She yawns, gives birth to a sparrow,
and the bird staggers upward
to the fence, battered
by its own breath,
its feathers rumpled and glistening,
its black eyes blinking back the new light.

Prayer

Brian Barker

—after Adam Zagajewski

God, give us a little presence—

Help us to remember
the wind in the weeds, the sparrows
alive in the scalded parking lot—

May the common miracle of rain
subdue the desert and the suburb—

In strangers let us recognize
ourselves:
    blood, longing, laughter,

and grief, that dark unnavigable ravine—

Help us to live between the wing
and the shadow of the wing—

Give us one more dawn—

This time we will rise in the cold
and carry you, a simple pebble,
beneath our tongues.

Seizure
Bill Hemminger

> *"Heaven blazing into the head"*
> *William Butler Yeats, "Lapis Lazuli"*

Down he fell; his eyes faced inward; words
collapsed. The little boy lay writhing on
the floor. A "petit mal," so care-givers
were told to let it run its course, a nervous
storm of motion. Circuits twitched in lobes
called temporal, where chemistry and world
collide, where neuro-transmitters,
undisciplined, rush through the landscape of
the brain that's lost control, a mind gone extraordinary. Would the boy report a mystic
meeting with a being great and caring—
or just euphoria beyond all words?

Now Helen's seventy years old, but she
bent down, stretched out her legs to make a human
fence that caught his flailing arms. The cosmic-
mental sparks subsided; then the boy
regained his outward sight, stood up, looked out.

Let me give you a hand, Helen, the little
Dostoevsky said. His brain's electric
grid restored but truly moved by light
of generous intention, wholly human,
he stooped to help the woman up.

Thought of the Week
E.R.Baxter III

EIGHTH GRADE METAL shop was a primitive little grotto in North Junior High School, on the ground floor, rear of the building, designed to prepare us for the factories or the trades to which most of us would graduate after high school. There might have been a single power source, one huge electric motor whose energy was distributed around the shop by horizontal shafts and levers that engaged an assortment of lathes, drill presses, milling machines, band saws, and other machinery by pulleys and long leather belts that at least in one place ran to a pulley at the tin ceiling, twelve feet above us. Gas flames pulsated bright orange from a series of small kilns that cradled the blunt heads of soldering irons ready for use, handles protruding over the bench. Against one wall were racks holding lengths of cold rolled steel in varying diameters, sheets of galvanized tin, shimmering new tin, other steel stock. There were dozens of unsafe conditions in plain sight, but OSHA had not yet been born, so they'd have to wait twenty years to be violations: exposed gears, sharp edges and corners waiting to slice thighs and wrists open, to gouge eyes out, tear fingers off, soldering irons just a few degrees below red hot, able to burn to the bone, leather belts whirling, blurred, waiting to grab a pants leg or shirt sleeve and run a limb around a pulley.

By all rights, we should have gone limping into ninth grade with eye patches, with crooked and scarred fingers, singed hair, puckered burn scars, the pink rat tracks of newly healed forearm stitches. But we did not. We came through unscathed. We loved it there in metal shop because we were in the eighth grade and we were immortal.

Mr. M., the shop teacher, who wore a suit, white shirt and tie, imagining he was the foreman, or the teacher, which he was, routinely said, in a gravelly voice, "Okay, boys, keep working. I'll be back in a few minutes." This meant at least a half hour, since he was off to visit his sweetie, a woman who taught in one of the upstairs classrooms. This was the signal for us to start chasing one another with hot soldering irons, to spit on torn scraps of paper and stick them onto the racing leather belts, and for one or two of the adventurous to grab hold of the belt speeding to the ceiling pulley, and rise up, letting go at the last instant to drop back to the floor. They were grabbing it before it grabbed them.

We all put in a lot of time doing our milling assignments, band sawing, and knurling exercises, and into soldering little deformed sugar scoops together from patterns we'd cut from tin and bent according to directions. These scoops our mothers dutifully plunged into the sugar containers at home, in spite of the lumpy solder and beads of hardened flux stuck like amber on the internal seams. That is, all of us but one of our classmates,

Bill L., who once he discovered he could turn out ball-peen hammer heads and handles on the lathe, went at it as if he were on piece work. No sugar scoops for him. If Mr. M. was out of the shop for forty-five minutes, Bill L. could make a ball-peen hammer, beautiful, perfect diamond knurling on the handle, the whole tool emery-clothed to a silver sheen. He made about a dozen of these, different sizes, during our metal shop weeks.

The last of these was a fourteen incher which, very much against the rules, he smuggled out of school as he had the rest of them, shoved handle first down inside the front of his pants, the hammer head held by the belt, his untucked shirt hanging over it. This last one he revealed to several of us as we walked home together after school, extracting it slowly, still keeping it partly concealed by his shirt. We all greatly admired the perfect gleaming workmanship of the hammer, the nerve it took to keep making them under Mr. M's nose and Bill L's successful thievery. We never told anyone, of course, because we were all from the same tool-poor neighborhood. I'm only telling now because so many years have passed. Bill L. and I lost touch shortly after Junior High. He went on through school to become a math teacher, I heard, of all things, and has since died. He's beyond all prosecution, now.

I sometimes wonder what became of his collection of ball-peens. Were they passed on to his children? Did he have any children? Did the hammers go in a garage sale for fifty cents each? Did anyone know their history? Do they languish still in a dusty toolbox somewhere? Rust has certainly dulled them, which might have started even weeks after they were made, because the steel we used was especially susceptible to the slightest moisture.

~~~

Whatever their fate, I still think of Bill L. whenever someone asks me, "How's your hammer hanging?" The "g" on "hanging" is never acknowledged by a real speaker of American English, naturally. It's "How's yer hammer hangin?" And if you're now beginning to think that I'm gradually working my way around to telling you how my hammer's hangin, you've got, as my father used to say, another think coming. That's my business.

~~~

I will tell you, however, the creation of the most enduring and valuable memory from eighth-grade metal shop was incidental, conveyed by a curious little icon of American advertising that is still with us today all across the nation, unhappily spread widely and grown large. But the message was the thing, after all, perhaps the most important thing I learned in Junior High or in any school thereafter, not that I realized it then, or have followed its guiding light since. Nevertheless, I look back to recognize the tiny doorway that opened to a different path, even if I've failed to walk it. And there's no reason I shouldn't pass it on.

High on the shop wall, about six feet to the left of where Mr. M. had positioned his desk, was an example of sheet metal work that some earlier student had made—or because it was especially well done, perhaps Mr. M. had crafted it himself. He never pointed it out to us, but we passed it each day as we entered the shop and again on our way out.

It was a model of a billboard, the edges folded to make a frame, about eight inches long and five high. From the top edge, supported by gracefully curved steel rods as slim as pencil lead, two small metal cones about half the size of thimbles pointed their wide ends at the face of the billboard. They were supposed to suggest spotlights, which they did, and had been neatly fashioned with one solder joint each, though they had not been wired with actual tiny bulbs. The tin of the entire piece had darkened over the years. Across the top of the billboard were words, the letters formed of melted solder, which read "Thought of the Week."

The face of the billboard had been cleverly slotted to hold a rectangle of paper on which the "thought of the week" would be printed. This paper could be easily changed. During the months we spent in metal shop, however, the words remained the same, printed in ink on paper that had yellowed with age. The words were "Read Good Books." They may have been printed there with the best of intentions when the billboard was brand new.

The students who noticed made fun of it because it never changed. We didn't realize that of all the "thoughts of the week" that could have been there, "Read Good Books" was clearly the best, even if the paper had yellowed and a fine dust had settled over it all. The dark and empty little spotlights were appropriate since the words themselves provided the illumination. If you followed their advice you would have your own thoughts of the week, or the month, or year for all the years of your life and there'd be no need to be rushing up to the billboard each week to see what the oracle had left.

So there you have it, and you can blow off this "thought of the week" on your own, for being obvious, commonplace, mundane, etc., even while you affirm its wisdom. Of course, you say, "Read Good Books," everyone knows that. Well, then, I have a question for you. If you believe "Read Good Books" is such a great thought, then why the hell are you reading this one?

~~~

What? You're going to try to squirm out of it by noting it doesn't say "Read Only Good Books"? Shame on you.

~~~

Thought of the week on billboards: they are visual pollution, omnipresent blotches along the roadsides and byways of our nation in growing numbers that could be nearing three quarters of a million in the near future. There were an estimated 500,000 of them in 1997. Some of us have trained ourselves not to notice them at all, as if they were floaters in the eye, some find them a distraction, and others see them as intrusive, demanding attention and blocking what might otherwise be a more natural view. It's time for them to go. Pass the necessary laws, arrange reparation for the billboard corporations and put thousands of people to work dismantling, transporting, and relocating them.

We've got enough billboards to build a wall one hundred feet high along the remaining 1300 of the 2000 miles of the United States-Mexico border. What's this half-hearted 700 mile effort? Aren't we the most powerful nation on earth? There's the Great Wall of China, the Berlin Wall, the wall that Israel is building, though some call it a "fence." We deserve to have our own wall, our own national monument of embarrassment and shame. When we fail to solve human problems of national, cultural, and economic complexity, then we should build a wall, an actual world representation of the invincible walls in our minds, and a damn big one, too.

A hundred feet high and 2000 miles long seems about right--it'd be visible from outer space. It'd be a tourist attraction. Loudspeakers spaced every five hundred feet could blare out Pink Floyd's "The Wall" continuously, twenty-four hours a day, louder on holidays. Terrorists would no longer have free passage in or out of the United States. It would inspire drug smugglers to new levels of creativity. We could sell naming rights to the wall. Since its components would have already been designed for such use, we could sell advertising space on it. Job listings could be posted on the Mexican side. The spotlights could be rewired and illumination of the whole wall achieved with solar panels and wind generators. This would provide a wonderful testing and demonstration site for the companies that manufacture such alternative energy devices.

Thousands of people would be employed in the wall construction: design engineers, carpenters, masons, concrete finishers, iron workers, electricians, laborers, and others. Agreements could be forged that would result in the hiring of a significant percent of Mexican workers, with union membership, wages, and benefits, of course. Even before the wall was completed it would be slowing the influx of immigrants by providing jobs on the border. Robert Frost, whose 1914 poem "Mending Wall" says that good fences make good neighbors, may have said it best, don't you think? Or is it possible you have misunderstood the poem? You haven't read it? You've forgotten Read Good Books already? "Mending Wall" also says that something doesn't like a wall.

In any case, the billboard wall would be one of those win, win, win, win, win situations we keep hearing about. You can probably think of dozens of other benefits. Perhaps the most significant, however, would be the opportunity it would provide for the President of Mexico—who, at a media conference in 2087, would stand in front of the wall, faced by cameras and microphones—to intone, dramatically, imperiously, cunningly, self-righteously, petulantly, and demandingly, "*Estoy hablando al Presidente de los Estados Unidos. ¡Tira esta pared!*"

~~~

The total elimination of billboards from American landscapes will probably never be achieved. To reach compromise between the opposing groups that will inevitably arise, such as Burn All Billboards (BAB) and Save our Billboards (SOB), provisions will probably have to be made for some of them, say 1000, to continue to exist. A newly formed governmental agency, Federal Exemptions for Billboard Art (FEBA) would make final decisions about which should survive based on historical significance or exceptional artistic value. One or more billboards on Route 66, for example, might qualify on the basis of location and time in service. This was the route, after all, where millions got their kicks, and some recognition needs to be paid. All the billboards that remained would be required to fit into two categories with regard to their displays: 1) public service announcement, or 2) reproductions of fine art, traditional or contemporary. Citizens would be able to petition FEBA with recommendations.

None of this will happen anytime soon, of course. Children entering kindergarten this year will be collecting Social Security checks before this plan gets underway. I have, nevertheless, started a rough draft of a petition to FEBA, to recommend the preservation of a billboard I favor.

It's located on the right side of the I-190 in Niagara County, New York, as the driver heads south toward the Grand Island Bridge. It's mounted on a single high pedestal in front of the remnants of a woods where I used to hunt years ago. There are no words on the billboard, nothing blatantly advertised. It's high enough for the sky to be a backdrop in the driver's vision and the billboard itself presents a background of blue that on a good day matches the blue of the real sky. White clouds shaped like buffalo drift across the blue of the billboard. The memories of all the vanished buffalo have been reborn, resurrected there from the artist's vision.

You probably remember how, when you were a child, the clouds took on shapes of fantastic and wonderful creatures, faces, outstretched arms, dragons that transformed themselves or fell to pieces as you gazed. You remember how mare's tails swept across the sky. You haven't got time for that shit anymore, do you? You're all grown up now. You'd plunge off the highway at 70 mph, still gazing, late for work for sure. That's why we need that buffalo cloud sky billboard, to remind us of what we've lost. We need to preserve at least a quick look at that mystical rectangle of sky, that doorway in the real, imagined, remembered world.

To Fellow Poets
Jeff Hardin

Seemingly, so many of us *want* despair,
as though from the fits of a heart's dark brooding
wisdom must emerge, truth wrenched free
from the torque of staring straight into loss.
Are we burnt out yet on being burnt out?
I was reading the other night when out of nowhere
the thought occurred: "I miss those ancient poets
who wrote without irony about the dew."
I guess I'm asking could we be naïve enough
to be naïve again. I guess I'm saying, "Yes."

A Study of Despair

Jeff Hardin

A boy, my Papaw dove along the ground
to seize the tails of snakes
        and fling them at the sky.
Toward the end, he said his death
        was just an arm's-length out ahead.

The woman struck today was pregnant,
pushing a stroller to beat the rain.
        In death, I hope she's
absent-minded and can't recall the mist
        that washed her infant's face.

The painter makes a study of despair,
though when he sleeps,
        the colors rearrange themselves
and look like joy, which the buyer drives
        two nails to hold in place.

I've never comprehended how that
one magnolia tucked behind the others
        posed a single bloom
nor why I happened past, beleaguered,
        as it writhed and argued with the wind.

Some say our prayers are commentaries on the end
of time. Before this stacks of books
        I hold just one, a thin volume,
though a lifetime won't be long enough
        to breathe its every page.

Black Bruise
Brent Fisk

A crow's call, half cackle, half cough.
Great clouds of them mass in oaks and walnuts,
give a harsh voice to hollow trees.
They are the shadow we cast on the sky.
On asphalt they snap up red meat in their beaks.
When they lift, ratty and tattered, to arc above
the lumbering train, the slow bend of rail ties,
only the corn whispers of winter.
Black poppy seeds, almost blue,
wheel over December's flagging rye,
and a blur edges the woods off east,
the anvil of a thundercloud rising.
I have sparks in my heart
and a remnant of crow feather
between my dream-clenched teeth.
I wake to the sound of a caw dying away
like a church bell rung at the outskirts
of empty Sunday sleep.

Scarecrows
James Scruton

You never see them anymore
in fields; they've shambled off
the farms, retired now
to front-porch fall tableaux
or just shadows of their former selves
in backyard gardens,
pie pans and pinwheels flashing
in the sunshine around them
like fast, newfangled traffic.

But I miss those bucketheads,
those strawmen at attention
in overalls and tattered flannel,
broomhandle arms fixed always
in that same cockeyed salute.

And I wish some spring
they'd make a comeback,
somehow pull themselves together
and take their beanpole places after all
the planting's done, a countryside
of humble sentinels again,
a host of patchwork knights to tilt
at the inscrutable, circling crows.

Grace

James Scruton

This late December afternoon
the snow is so fine coming down
I can barely see it through the window,
unconvinced until I'm outside
catching it like salt across
the dark palms of my gloves.

It's coming down as a friend of mine says
grace does, on the just
and unjust alike, asked for or not,
believed in or doubted. And who am I
to say he's wrong, to tell him

that faith is one more word
for need so great it must be holy,
a desire for truth or peace
or another life in which to find them—
or more often just for love,
prayer enough in any wind, any season.

Migrations
Richard Cecil

Nobody cares about your October leaves,
which take you back to grade school, where you stared
out high windows at the playground squirrels
gathering fallen walnuts in their jaws
while Sister Joseph silently crept up
behind and poked her yardstick in your back.
Others are staring at their October leaves
and wondering what happened to their cap gun
with fake-pearl plastic Lone-Ranger handgrips
that they used to aim at squawking birds
ganging in their back yard's maple branches.
When they pulled the trigger—POP—the flock
took off and circled chimneys, then flew south,
as they once wished that they could, and still wish:
ditch math homework, go AWOL from their job,
surrender to their migratory instinct.

Instead, nostalgia grips them like the flu—
not the deadly kind that's killing geese
and pretty soon will thin the human race,
just the low-grade-fever kind that slows
your brain way down and makes your body weak.
Lazy as you are, how did you manage
to cross the desert of your life to get here?
Subtracting childhood years when you were pushed
by parents and teachers towards your lonesome future,
you're left with arid stretches that you crossed
without assistance towards your goal: Today.
And all the children who took off with you
who haven't yet been shot down have arrived
by different paths to perch here and admire
like you, October's burning leaves awhile,
then fly off separately into the smoke.

The Redwood Brigade
Fred Haefele

EUREKA, CALIFORNIA, MARCH 17th: On a sodden, fog-clotted North Coast morning, a trio of hard-hatted tree-climbers rappeled leisurely down the trunk of a two-hundred foot redwood older than Christianity. Their goal was to evict a slender, spectacled young tree-sitter known as "Remedy."

For team leader Eric Schatz, a Eureka native, it was the shakedown test of America's first professional tree-sitter extraction team.

For Remedy, 26, of Mount Pleasant, Michigan, the eviction would prevent the celebration of her first anniversary aboard the 13-feet-in-diameter giant the tree-sitters call "Jerry."

A hundred or so feet below Remedy's 4x8 tarpaulin-covered redoubt was a melange of 15 Humboldt County Sheriffs, seven correctional staff, four Highway Patrolmen, numerous security employees of Pacific Lumber Company (known as PalCo, owners of the tree), various press crews and a kind of intersectarian group of environmental activists calling themselves "The Forest Defenders."

~~~

Had they been privy to the conversation above them, they would have heard what, according to both extractor and extractee, was a philosophical debate of near surreal rectitude:

Schatz: "Good morning, Remedy. Hey—while I greatly admire your principles and determination to protect this tree, it's my duty to inform you that this *is* private property and you're trespassing."

Remedy: "Good morning, Climber Eric. While I appreciate your coming all the way up to apprise me of this, in good conscience I can't abandon this ancient being to PalCo's cavalier and non-sustainable harvest policies."

Or something like that.

After a couple hour's discussion, Remedy at last slipped her hands into her "lock box," (a home-made manacle chained around Jerry's trunk) and proceeded to take herself hostage.

The Extraction Team then hauled a compressed-air-powered grinder up on a rope. As the grinder ground and Remedy's manacles heated up, Schatz stood by, cooled her arms with Perrier. Hours later, the manacle severed, the climbers handcuffed Remedy with plastic ties, strapped her into an evacuation harness. Schatz lifted her in his arms and the two were lowered gently to the ground on one-half-inch 16-strand braided nylon rope. According to at least one witness, they cut a dashing figure.

To PalCo's way of thinking, this engagement was probably a smashing success—just the type of orderly *pro forma* extraction (or "rescue," as PalCO describes them) the embattled company had hoped for.

On the other hand, the Forest Defenders were *bummed*. By the time Remedy and Wren, another sitter, were brought down and packed in a sheriff's car, the activists attempted to block the road, and a baton-and-pepper-spray fracas erupted. It lasted ten minutes, resulted in several arrests.

When I spoke with Remedy a few days later, her anniversary spoiled, she reported glumly that she was treated well enough "up there":

"So they weren't goons or anything, the Palco guys?"

"No, they were very smooth. And Eric—well, he'll charm the pants right off you."

"Does that mean he was gentlemanly?"

"Oh, extremely so. Outwardly. But inwardly? Inwardly, he's *sick*."

~~~

Freshwater, a steep, heavily-logged drainage about three miles north of Eureka, has for nearly a decade been an epicenter in the fight to save Humboldt County's remaining Old Growth trees. The acreage, thanks to the Greenwood Heights Road, is easily accessible to loggers, activists and media alike, resulting in an on-going melodrama in which both trees and sitters have taken starring roles. (For the most part in this production, PalCo has played the villain.)

~~~

At first just an annoyance, the un-harvested redwoods the sitters occupy have become an increasing source of frustration to the financially strapped company. Until recently, they could do little about it. Then, in early March, the company got a restraining order from a federal judge allowing them to physically remove the sitters.

This was far easier said then done.

That's when they turned to Schatz, a local arborist.

One of maybe a dozen old growth specialists in the country, Schatz climbs these giants routinely to prune away deadwood or storm damage. Or he may rig and remove tons of rotted tree top hanging over a million-dollar home. All these operations he will perform without ruffling a shingle, harming the tree or fracturing his skull.

Schatz's been doing this for 31 years, a span of time over which he estimates he's climbed a hundred thousand vertical feet, or well beyond the stratosphere. Part of his skill as a big tree climber is to take something that appears insanely hazardous, make it seem a perfectly reasonable, even quotidian thing to do.

It isn't.

Professionals at Schatz's level have long understood that macho has no place in their world. Their survival depends on cool, not daring; caution, not swagger. These were exactly the intangible he looked for when he first formed his team.

To qualify, team members needed a minimum of ten years' old-growth experience, plus extensive training in alpine rescue, non-violent problem solving and crowd psychology. For starters.

On a rainy Friday night, I met Schatz and an E-team climber called Ox at a Eureka coffee shop. They were cordial but extremely wary. They told me, point blank, they didn't trust the press. To make matters worse, an activist called "Tree" threw himself under Schatz's Suburban on his way over to meet with me. Schatz barely avoided running him over.

I stirred my coffee. "Are you guys still rattled?"

The two exchanged glances. Schatz is wiry, compact, a youthful 46 year old with a Guardsman's mustache. Ox is tall and powerfully built, a soft spoken, 50-year-old grandfather.

"More and more," Ox reflected, "'rattled' is a way of life around here."

Here's how Schatz's operation works:

The E-team (as they call themselves) totals six climbers, generally three to a tree. Their ground support group—belayers, suppliers and such —might include another half dozen, plus whatever law enforcement seems appropriate. In theory, the team will stay operational until the situation is resolved. They do not rely heavily on stealth. Because of sophisticated activist technology (cell-phones, computers, walkie-talkies) and because rigging a big tree ascent takes time, the element of surprise is pretty much eliminated.

"Hell," Schatz told me. "They not only know exactly when we're coming, they know us all by name!"

At the occupied tree, the E-Team uses a cross-bow to shoot a monofilament line through a crotch 100 feet up. With this, they haul up a climbing rope, rig it for single line ascent, then one by one, head up into the canopy.

"Every tree's different," says Schatz. "We try to avoid coming up under the sitter's platforms but lots of times we can't. And when that happens, well, that's always dicey. They say they're non-violent, but ... let's just say, some take the idea more seriously than others."

In truth, never is the E-team more vulnerable than at this point, and their safe ascent depends entirely on a kind of gentlemen's agreement with the sitters that all encounters *will* be non-violent.

Seeking the high ground, E-teamers climb to a point well above the activists. They pick a staging area, belay themselves, set their evacuation rigging, usually a pair of 300-foot descent lines run through alloy pulleys and anchored to a belaying device.

Then, like an aerial boarding party, the team rappels to the sitter's bivouac below, where the first order of business is a kind of on-the-spot evaluation: Does the sitter pose a physical threat? Is the sitter hypothermic? Stoned? Mal-nourished? *Rational?*

While Schatz and Ox talked easily about procedure, technique and equipment, and while they were justifiably proud of their safety record to date, they talked less easily about the activists and their *modus operandi*. These were described in tense, sobering dispatches: marginal clothing, low-protein diets in cold, wet weather. Limited climbing skills, lots of dope and most ominously, lots of makeshift safety gear. Since 1998, two sitters have died from questionable belays; another was severely injured.

But most troubling to the team is that they never know how a sitter will react to their presence—that is, how far he or she might go to make a stand.

One young woman stripped naked when the team arrived. They waited till the cold weather forced her to dress.

~~~

Schatz recounts, unprintably, the time another sitter doused him with a water bucket.

Things, in the E-team's view, keep escalating. A few days after my visit, Schatz called to tell me a contingent from Earth Liberation Front made an impromptu visit to his home, where they informed Schatz, cryptically, that whatever he did to the treesitters, they were prepared to do to him.

Then there was "Phoenix," who slipped past security, made his way into the outer branches of one tree, free-climbed over a hundred feet straight up, right past the E-Team, already landed on the sitter's platform.

"He was headed for our belays when I tackled him," said Schatz. "Ox and I wrestled him down and sat on him, at which point the kid went mental. He said he was suicidal. He shook us off, made a dive for the edge of the platform, got halfway off before we could grab his legs and stop him. You can't tell me that guy wasn't smoking SOMEthing—the way he fought us? And that was after climbing a hundred feet straight up!"

In the course of our conversation, I avoided asking Schatz and Ox any kind of Big Question. In truth, I was far less interested in their views on Old Growth harvest than I was in the climbing/rescue skills that allow the safe extraction of an unwilling tree sitter from a 200-foot tree. Still, by evening's end, the two remained sober and wary. As if the interview was a kind of sucker punch waiting to happen.

~~~

Before I left Eureka, I was invited by Remedy and the Forest Defenders to view the video they'd made of a March 19th E-Team operation. I was received hospitably by them at their Freshwater digs, where I sprawled on the living room floor to watch it amid a welter of dogs, tea-mugs and amped-up activists.

Leaving aside all the oft-expressed, fervently held opinions of both sides in this consuming and fulminatory environmental debate, if you chose to view Remedy's extraction as a model of big-tree decorum (as I did), the operation revealed by the Forest Defenders' footage was significantly messier, vastly more frightening.

A new sitter, "Mystique," re-occupied Remedy's old tree, and the footage opened with her a hundred feet above the old bivouac, bear-hugging the tree's ten-inch diameter top, apparently un-belayed.

We then cut to Schatz, working his way up from below. Depending on who you listen to, he has either provoked a game of Redwood chicken, or Mystique has blundered into a jam of her own making and Schatz is performing a rescue.

Though the crowd below is raucous—hazing Schatz, shouting encouragement to Mystique—the canopy drama is unmiked, silent. The video is overexposed, so the climbers are in silhouette, like puppets in a Balinese shadow play.

Schatz draws close to Mystique's perch and stops.

The two seem to talk.

Then the crowd goes silent. Mystique, fresh out of vertical, veers abruptly to the horizontal, edges her way out a branch the diameter of a base ball. She shuffles a couple feet then freezes.

Schatz speaks to her. Whatever he says, it has the wrong effect, and he watches helplessly while Mystique, in the name of protection, tosses an anemic prussic cord over a remarkably unsubstantial looking sucker, hangs onto it like a sub-way strap while she edges straight for the Void. A bad move in any tree, at 200 feet, it's the worst you can make.

Schatz climbs level with Mystique, belays himself with his lanyard. They talk briefly.

Something gives way and Mystique pitches forward, grabs a handful of redwood twigs to stop her fall.

Now the crowd comes alive. They bad-mouth Schatz, tell Mystique they love her, that the trees love her, too. "Be strong," they tell her, "Be strong!" There's swearing, weeping, imprecations. Someone calls 911. Except for some random ululation, it sounds quite a bit like Friday Night SmackDown. Yet the pair up the tree is breath-taking; like spirits, cast in shadow. Anything can happen now.

Two hundred feet above the forest floor with no place left to go, their conversation looks feverish, strangely intimate.

According to Schatz, it went like this:

"Listen to me. We're in a bad spot. You go out further, it's pure suicide. You're a tough cookie, an awesome climber and now everyone knows it. You've got nothing left to prove."

According to Mystique, it was like this:

"Hey. You fall out of this tree now, neither me or my crew's responsible. We'll testify it was suicide, plain and simple."

Oddly enough, both parties agree on what happens next:

Schatz doffs his safety glasses. He's crying.

"Listen," he says "I'm really afraid right now. I don't want to die today and I don't want you to die, either. Please. Help me get us out of this mess."

Mystique, crying too, agrees, allows Schatz to loop a lanyard around her and gently pull her in.

Back on earth, the arboreal *rapprochement* disappears like vapor: Mystique claims she was struck in the mouth by a carabineer during her evacuation; that a petulant E-Team lowered her to the ground "by my chest."

~~~

Before I packed to leave, I spoke to Andrew Edwards, reporter for the *North Coast Journal*, a local weekly. He was convinced that the climbers and sitters had a pretty good rapport. He said he'd seen them joke around, try to recruit each other, share Powerade and climbing lore.

In the trees, things seemed to work, he said. "It's the crowd on the ground that's weird ... that's where things go sour."

It reminded me of something Remedy said, when I asked her what it was like, back on terra firma after a year in the tree.

She shook her head, smiled vaguely. "It's amazing how good it smells up there, she said. "And how much the ground really stinks. "

BOOK REVIEWS

Silkie
by Anne-Marie Cusac
Many Mountains Moving Press, 2007
84 pages
$ 14.95

Reviewed by Gregory Hagan

The Celtic-Norse folk ballad "The Great Silke of Sule Sherry" rocks the waves on the shores of the Orkney Islands. The story is rather simple, shrouded in myth and magic. A young maiden falls in love with a silkie, a creature with the power to shape-shift from a seal at sea to a man on land after he has shed his seal skin. The maiden then has a child by him, and he promises to return for his child after seven years with a bag of gold. In some versions, the silkie also predicts that the maiden will marry a seal hunter who will kill both him and the child. Ann Marie Cusac explores this myth in her second collection of poetry, Silkie, a narrative sequence, and in so doing creates a book that, like the silkie , "leaps like a white wing."

Cusac's work has appeared in *Poetry*, the *Iowa Review,* the *Crab Orchard Review*, and other magazines. Her first collection of poetry, *The Mean Days,* appeared in 2001. She is a former Wallace Stegner Fellow at Stanford University and is currently a contributing writer for *The Progressive* and a professor in Communication at Roosevelt University.

Dulsie, Cusac's version of the young woman who falls in love with the silkie, is disarmingly sweet but "wild enough / to sleep alone on the beach," not once but many times, and seals "can spot a girl like that," a young woman whose body throws off a certain light. A silkie fathers her child. In this act of passion, the silkie does not seduce her violently like Leda's swan, but rather softly, with "the sound of lapping waves" and "the sand / giving under her shoulders."

Cusac's poems can be gentle and charming and also frightening as a fairy tale. Listen to the suitor-seal when he speaks to Dulsie: "You'll have our daughter for seven years. I'll come back for her / and pay you for your trouble." The central figure, Dulsie, perhaps at most a high school senior when the sequence of poems begins, is electric, ephemeral, enigmatic and myth herself. Her hair flames, and she calls men and boys to lust. She even leaps fires on the beach "as if lifted on silk." Dulsie's father doesn't understand her, and neither do we. He says, "I stare and see just motion / as if darkness hurries down the staircase." Scott Boyd, a fellow classmate of Dulsie's, sees her this way: "her current / still travels across us / the way a rank vine infects a wall." Dulsie is bitter, tough and fragile, all at the same time. When the silkie departs, "she shivers," and so do we. Dulsie is attracted to that which she cannot ultimately possess, and we are drawn to her like the silkie

Cusac creates lyrical magic in the poem "silkie song." Here the silkie speaks of Dulsie: "She flames like a window at evening / her hair the color of late sunset / so low and molten it drips into the water." Like Dulsie's body, Cusac's poems cast a certain transcendent light, allowing them to reveal the traumatic disappearance of the self. Her poems also explore transformation and the hunger for transformation. In the poem, "if she could change," Dulsie and the silkie stand before one another:

> But the night she really tries,
> when he begins to shudder and shift
> and she runs to him, and pulls him
> heavily onto her, willing whatever alchemy
> makes him differ so from himself
> to change her, too, his torso pounds
> the breathing out of her lungs.
> The new face tips and takes her in,
> surprised, indifferent.

Few of these poems stand alone but instead are connected with a silk thread to create a work akin to a novella often punctuated by the brutal thread of realism. Cusac sometimes excerpts comments from seal hunters. For example, Jack Nicholson of St. Paul's Island recounts: "We had a sheath knife in our belt and a club—and when you see a seal you'd club him across the nose and sell him." This cruel reality opens the door into the realm of myth. When Dulsie finds herself with child, her "monster, darling," she thinks, "she and the life swimming inside her / are one more trick / of fecundity?"

In this collection, you will find love, and the need for love; you will find grief; you will find the possibility of another world; you will encounter desire and death. One August summer as I crossed over from Portland, Maine on the ferry to Peaks Island, I gave little thought to "The Great Silke of Sule Sherry" while seals with all too human eyes bobbed their heads in Casco Bay, their curious eyes following the human cargo. As Joseph Campbell has said, "Myths are clues to the spiritual potentialities of human life." Cusac interweaves big poems in Silkie, and the sum is greater than the parts.

Things Kept, Things Left Behind
by Jim Tomlinson
University of Iowa Press, 2006
153 pages
$15.95 (paper)

Reviewed by Morgan Williams

Every story in Jim Tomlinson's *Things Kept, Things Left Behind* throbs with a sense of regret for the things that went wrong. Tomlinson's characters are very much aware of themselves and of what they have done: they want to make up for past mistakes, rise above their past lives, or just come to terms with what has happened. Overall, the collection has a rather melancholy feel. In each story, a past decision or mistake comes back to haunt the central character or characters, forcing new decisions on them.

Some of these choices are made in the innocence of youth. "Prologue (two lives in letters)," one of the most intricate pieces in the book, begins with the chance meeting of two students, Davis Menifee from Kentucky and Claire Lyons from Connecticut, at a summer conference. In the first letter, Davis professes to be "anxious for school to be over, summer done, and the rest of my life to begin." The couple go their separate ways, but their connection and their correspondence continue over 34 years, through the Kennedy assassination, the Vietnam War, and the various trials of their lives and chosen professions. In the end, many things have changed, and their lives have veered sharply away from the paths they planned for. But Tomlinson allows them to roll with the punches and to pick themselves up. The final letter, which is Claire's, ends with "For five minutes, no more, I will gaze at the cloud and the contrail tapestry drifting overhead, and when that time is up, I will brush myself off and move on."

In some stories, the choices are made by people who are trying, however hopelessly, to get their lives back in order. In "First Husband, First Wife," the protagonists break the law in an attempt to reconnect with each other one more time. In this story, as in many others in the book, the people involved find themselves somewhat older, with their formative mistakes behind them. Their marriage is over, and even the theft the story centers on lies in the past. But Jerry and Cheryl aren't devoid of a certain kind of hope. In the hotel room where they go to celebrate his release from prison, Jerry is already planning his next great scheme to repair their lives, thinking: "…maybe he'd get into ginseng, what Shuey called 'sang.' Foreigners paid a small fortune for a wild-grown root shaped like an animal… His wasted months at Blackburn were ending today. His life was starting again. This time he'd get it right."

One of Tomlinson's major triumphs with these stories is that he does not allow his characters to slip down into self-pity. They are much more resilient than that, and there is a strong theme of prevailing over hardships. While the major events, in some cases the most important events, of their lives have passed, they commit themselves to the present, opening themselves up to the possibility of a moment of revelation. As in life, sometimes all that is needed to solidify years of thought is one event. Tomlinson artfully brings his characters to these events in a way that allows readers to feel as if they have made the same journey, in the space of only a few pages.

Things Kept, Things Left Behind is Jim Tomlinson's first book-length collection of short stories, and his first independent publication. Tomlinson has published stories in *Arts Across Kentucky*, as well as in *The Pinch, Bellevue Literary Review* and *Five Points*. *Things Kept, Things Left Behind* won The Iowa Short Fiction Award in 2006.

And The Sea
by Christopher Buckley
The Sheep Meadow Press, 2006
87 pages
$12.95 (paper)

Reviewed by Vince Tweddell

Hints of God appear often in Christopher Buckley's fourteenth book of poetry *And The Sea*. Buckley's God, though, is not one forced upon readers, but rather encountered simply as a part of everyday life—in thinking, dreaming, remembering, working. Sometimes Buckley seems unflinching in his faith, and at other junctures, we wonder if the God in these poems represents in some form a show of slight bitterness.

The poet proves equally noncommittal on both fronts. "Unlike God, we have few disguises—finally,/we are so many minerals," he writes in "Photo Without Cap." In "Analects of the Essenes," he writes:

> Water lines on rock, the dry blood and breath of urns,
> The unanswered interrogative of the sky—God
> Can be seen as a white tail slipping over
>
> The sea, the water its own eternity beyond the shaking
> Faith of trees. A star burning above the voices
> Of the palms, the blurred scrolls of dawn.

The poetry in this collection spans a lifetime, from boyhood to manhood and in-between. We at times find ourselves admiring the landscape and lifestyle of a California childhood, and in the next instant, we are left to contemplate how these moments help or hinder in the evolution to adulthood. "Memory," the first poem of the collection, draws us into the mind of a boy and then shoots us to the man writing the poem:

> We didn't have the first idea about ideas,
> and, diving beneath kelp beds, shot the carefree fish
>   with our hand-sling spears and never gave
> a thought to what the trident symbolized–a soul
>   was only something in a catechism text,
>   an emptiness in the air we were never going to touch,
>   unlike the eucharist-white bones of the fish.

To illuminate his work, Buckley employs intense visuals—still shots of the ocean, birds chirping in a backyard or flapping through salty air above sandy beaches, lemon trees, misty ocean sprays, old family photographs and those of famous deceased poets. In "September," he paints this picture:

> Light sliced through eucalyptus, strained
> through construction paper clouds
>   cut out and pinned over the eastern ridge––
> shorthand of leaves on the asphalt,
>   dry mist of grass spun over the playing field.

And he ends "All Saint's Day" with this vision:

> All I need
> is time, a long lasting
> bit of it beyond
> the shadow-heavy roofs
> where the birds gather
> at this same hour each day—
> starlings, scrub jays, doves–
> for the last striations and
> instructions of the light,
> which are theirs forever....

Buckley's many formal choices symbolize the myriad answers to the questions this collection asks: *Am I a good person? Have I led a good life?* Poems in step lines such as "Waking Up in My Car at Miramar Point" and "Grey Evenings," prose poems such as "There," and "Spring Sabbatical," and poems in free-verse couplets such as "Philosophy" and "Mystery" all move through different methods to reach similar endings, stepping through the sometimes muddled, compact mass of words and ideas and beliefs to find a structure that works for an individual's daily life. And still the questions keep coming. Buckley does not offer concrete answers, and forever the wonder will remain, sitting under a God-soaked haze hanging over California.

In "Poem Beginning with a Line from Tu Fu," Buckley writes,

> I take an early drink,
>   and praise whatever is left
> of my Fate—
>   no different finally,
>   than anyone else's ...
> I have no idea what
>   I want now
>   beyond everything
> I've ever had
>   all over again ...

Despite a level of hardships and successes no more disappointing, nor uplifting than most, Buckley, now middle-aged, seems, like Tu Fu, at peace with a search that is sure to be fruitless, yet a search that must never end.

Dr. King's Refrigerator and Other Bedtime Stories
by Charles Johnson
Scribner, 2005
123 pages
$20.00

Reviewed by Daniel Dowell

One could safely say that no major publisher would have given *Dr. King's Refrigerator and Other Bedtime Stories* a second look if Charles Johnson weren't the author of such highly acclaimed works as *Oxherding Tale* and *Middle Passage* (which won the National Book Award). Full of parables, philosophical allegories, and anecdotes, Johnson's latest collection comprises a selection of self-indulgent shorts that often ask tough questions, but do so in ways unusual for a contemporary author. Luckily for readers (in this case, at least), marketing departments in the publishing world temporarily suspend their prejudices when it comes to literary big shots. *Dr. King's Refrigerator* fails to live up to the quality of Johnson's earlier works, but not all his experiments go awry. The result is a flawed but highly-readable, amusing, and disturbing book that turns expectations on their heads.

The opening story, "Sweet Dreams"—a futuristic Big Brother tale set in post-9/11 America—places the reader directly in the action via a second-person, present-tense point of view and serves as a ferry (think Willy Wonka) to the surreal dream world Johnson has created. "Cultural Relativity" and "The Gift of the Osuo" (arguably the centerpiece of the collection) qualify as out-and-out fables. The former, a prince-and-frog story, offers a rather simplistic and straightforward lesson in—you guessed it—cultural relativism, while the latter reads like one part morality tale and one part metaphysical treatise. "Dr. King's Refrigerator" and "The Queen and the Philosopher" fictionalize events in the lives of historical figures. "Executive Decision" (also in second-person and present tense, for effect) gives the reader an impossible choice: do you hire the perfect white interviewee or the near-perfect black interviewee, whose imperfections stem from the injustices Affirmative Action is supposed to rectify? "Better than Counting Sheep" takes an unexpectedly light-hearted, *Dilbert*-like jab at office life. The closing story, "Kwoon," emerges as the only conventional piece in the bunch.

In most of these stories, Johnson delivers the socio-political commentary and philosophical discourse one would expect from him, and, of course, most of the views presented are of a decidedly liberal bent. The opening story warns us of the dangers of governmental encroachment on our privacy in the name of "homeland security." "Cultural Relativity" reads like a myth invented to scare children into respecting societal differences. The title story examines the interconnectedness of all peoples.

In "Executive Decision," Johnson's stance on affirmative action appears less clear, as he wrestles with its practical implications. On the one hand, the whole point of such policies is to offset the effects of past and present discrimination. On the other hand, because of said discrimination, those who are its victim often prove less qualified in some way. He asks, "But except before the law, and in the eyes of God, are *any* two people truly equal?" The dilemma is further illustrated by an argument between two secondary characters borrowed from Melville, Nips and Turk:

> "You are not," pressed Nips, "concerned about discrimination?"
> "Oh, pshaw! We all discriminate, Nips! Every moment of every day we choose one thing rather than another on the

basis of our tastes, prejudices, and preferences. How else can we achieve life, liberty, and the pursuit of happiness? I remember that you, back in our school days, never deigned to direct your affections toward women taller than yourself or, for that matter, toward men. It's reasonable, I'm saying, to have likes and dislikes, and to act upon them ... "

Nips responds with a discussion of Rawls' ethics—the socially advantaged, he says, owe it to the less fortunate to try to balance things out. The epigraph, a quote from Kant, leads the reader to believe the author leans toward a particular viewpoint, but the feeling one gets by the end of the piece is that Johnson is not as sure as he would like to be.

The two main problems with this collection concern the intermittent quality of the work and the lack of thematic unity. While many stories are thought-provoking or, at least, entertaining, "Sheep" and "Kwoon" fall short on both accounts, the first because of its *Office Space* qualities and the second because of its sugary sweetness. And though the early stories share a dream-like quality, that tone comes and goes later on and disappears entirely by the end of the book. The thematically hit-and-miss nature of the collection is surely due to its being composed of mostly previously published works rather than pieces written specifically to fit the bedtime story mood. Whatever the reason, the result is that what starts off powerfully climaxes early and falls flat in the end.

Overall, *Dr. King's Refrigerator* is a mixed bag—some gems, some interesting rocks, and a few lumps of coal. However, if one can struggle through the lesser stories, the reward for such ardor is a nightmare that's hard to resist.

Saturday
by Ian McEwan
Random Houser, 2005
298 pages
$14.95 (paper)

Reviewed by Chris Meredith

Although set in London, *Saturday*, the latest novel from *Atonement*-author Ian McEwan, proves anything but specifically English. It relates the 24-hour odyssey of Henry Perowne, a brilliant neurosurgeon who, under McEwan's steady direction, becomes a more universally accessible character than his position might imply. In fact, via a brief glimpse into Perowne's life, we get something of an allegory of life in the post-9/11 world.

Saturday is, above all, a character's novel and, appropriately, McEwan portrays Perowne as a richly-layered character with a complex set of values. From the beginning, McEwan establishes Perowne as remarkably adept at his job ("He clipped the neck of a middle cerebral artery aneurysm—he's something of a master in the art"). Although Perowne's professional life is seemingly completely under his control, his family life is much more complicated, especially his relationship with his poet daughter Daisy, who views him as a bit of a philistine in matters outside of medicine.

Perowne remains uncertain about his feelings toward the impending invasion of Iraq and the massive protest to take place across the city. This uncertainty leads to a kind of indifference to the social unrest that surrounds him, a complacency disrupted by an unnerving encounter with Baxter, a bizarre diminutive man who assaults Perowne, but whose violent impulses Perowne attributes to Huntington's Disease. McEwan does not utilize the Baxter character as a traditional heavy. Rather, Baxter's mercurial nature, alternately sympathetic and terrifying, reflects the increasingly tumultuous nature of the city and the way it has begun to invade Perowne's consciousness, despite his attempts at imperviousness.

Although primarily a character study, *Saturday* becomes a surprisingly taut page-turner, particularly around the last 100 pages, as Baxter and his cronies break into Perowne's home and hold his family hostage. In one particularly chilling scene, Baxter forces Daisy to undress and recite some of her poetry. McEwan creates such an intense feeling of exposure and invasion that one can almost share Daisy's fear: "Daisy goes down faster now, pulling off her tights with an impatient gasp, almost tearing at them, then throwing them down. She's undressing in a panic ... "

Though the novel's climax assumes many elements of a thriller, McEwan does not give in to any form of sensationalism or contrivance. Instead, the tension created by the plot allows his various thematic concerns to come full circle. The issue of control, for example, reemerges when Perowne finds himself torn between maintaining control by protecting his family from a threat that has invaded their fairly insulated lives and, by helping Baxter receive the treatment he should have had years ago, maintaining the kind of control that he knows best: the control that only a renowned surgeon can feel. McEwan subtly parallels Perowne's dilemma with the broader political issues he presents: is it best to take a proactive approach to preventing violence, or is it better to try to avoid it altogether and possibly face the consequences later?

If the novel has a weakness, it may be that it is overloaded with political imagery and discourse. Although politics are an important element of the story, there are times when the references become heavy-handed and superfluous. The novel begins, for example, with Perowne rising from bed in a dream-like state and spotting a plane in flames that he assumes is going to crash. Although it turns out to be a minor incident, the image is obviously supposed to represent the lingering anxiety of 9/11. This development does not enhance the story as well as does the background of the war protest and feels rather unnecessary.

There are also times when the political debates, particularly between fence-sitting Perowne and the staunchly anti-war Daisy, go on too long and become a bit too involved for their purpose. Since this is not, after all, an overtly political novel, but rather one that uses politics to explore more basic human conflicts, these discussions sometimes knock the story out of focus.

Nevertheless, *Saturday* remains a most incisive study of life in the modern world and gives readers a compelling blend of rich characterization, emotional clarity, and tense plotting. Despite his brilliance, Henry Perowne is, in many ways, an ordinary man, striving to understand himself and his relationships both to those closest to him and to the world at large. The Saturday in question stands not simply as a day in the life of one man, but as a microcosm of the way we all live.

Poet's Choice
by Edward Hirsch
Harcourt, Inc., 2006
432 pages
$ 25.00

Reviewed by Kevin Marshall Chopson

Last year I had the pleasure of introducing Edward Hirsch at an "Author Strand" session of the 2006 convention of the National Council of Teachers of English. Hirsch began his presentation by reading from the introduction to *Poet's Choice*, calling it a "prayer." The actual opening lines constitute a direct address: "Sun-struck mornings, rainy afternoons, starry nights of poetry, come back to me now, remember me. Do not desert me, lifetime of encounters, lifelines, sentencings." In a prayer, one expresses thanks, acknowledges the spiritual strength of the creator, makes an appeal for continued blessings, calls for intervention. In *Poet's Choice*, Hirsch attempts to demonstrate the power individual poems and poets have upon us; he is reverent and thankful for the art that has sustained him throughout his whole life.

Poet's Choice encompasses 130 brief chapters, most of which originally appeared as newspaper articles in the *Washington Post Book World* after September 11, 2001. The order has been changed and some new pieces added but the intent is the same– to bring some order to the chaos. As Hirsch says, "... poetry sustains us in hard times." From entries on individual poets (e.g., Caedmon, Sappho, Rilke, Justice) to thematic chapters such as one on "The Ars Poetica," in which lines from Horace, Whitman, Marianne Moore, Hugh MacDiarmid, and Czeslaw Milosz all share the page, Hirsch attempts to get at the meaning, effectiveness, and purpose of it all—a common rhetorical investigation that here becomes delightfully informative. Chapters cut through time and place in order to allow a unique conversation among poems. As a bonus, the commentary itself is poetic in its language and potentially epiphanic on a personal level.

Everything is here in this text that is not wholly anthology, textbook, or collection of essays: extensive biography on Neruda, a classification of Mark Jarman's work ("God-haunted"), a quick lesson in form regarding Gerard Manley Hopkins (I learned what a curtal sonnet is, for instance). In the thematic chapters such as "Nightingales," "Women and War," "Insomnia," "Birth Poems," "Reading," "Nebraska Poetry" and "Farewell," sometimes who shows up in the discussion is predictable, sometimes a surprise. Ted Kooser is on The Plains, Whitman is everywhere. Each poem, poet, or theme receives a unique treatment.

The book is also divided squarely down the middle—sixty-five chapters in Part One, devoted to "international" poetry, and sixty-five chapters in Part Two, devoted to American poetry. We see the beginnings and the contemporary in both. "There is something bittersweet about [Radmila] Lazic's utterly convincing work, which has the texture of lived experience," Hirsch says of the relatively little known Serbian poet. "[She] writes as a feminist with a dark sense of humor and a surreal imagination, a woman forthright about her desires ('Let me get to the nitty-gritty,' the speaker announces in 'Dorothy Parker Blues.' 'I give you the visa / To my body—my homeland') and unsentimental about marriage." Similarly, he places the well-known American poet Gary Snyder on a larger stage. "The commitments and connections in Snyder's work are clear and precise," Hirsch says. "He is a singer of community. He speaks of three hundred million years ago and of the world right now."

This book covers a lot of ground, but Hirsch is a great teacher. Each chapter provides a little lesson, wonderfully crafted. His style is that of a warm, inviting mentor steeped in the ways of Socrates. The poems and ideas presented here ask questions. The experience of sitting under Hirsch's tutelage, book in hand, generates even more. May *Poet's Choice* meet with the great audience it deserves.

Let Me Explain
by Gaylord Brewer
Iris Press, 2006
104 pages
$ 14.00

Reviewed by Jenna Wright

In *Let Me Explain*, his sixth volume of poetry, Gaylord Brewer delivers a se-ries of apologias written over a period of more than two years. Within these apologias, the speakers defend, or at least feign to justify, their feelings *for* or *against* the subject identified in the title, whether it be a billowing curtain, the first day of school, a woman's ear, a martini glass, or America at war. *Let Me Explain* portrays much of the incongruity in life, and that incongruity generates the need for explanation. The explanations Brewer gives—at once simple and complex—prove biting at times but consistently tempered with compassion. In the poem "Apologia for the Bone Box," the speaker acknowl-edges, "When I became a child / I put away manly things." Still, he insists, "We need less gloom in the room / more light, less hell, more laughs." The poems in *Let Me Explain* convey "less gloom and more light."

The apologia, an ancient form for philosophical argumentation, establishes within the premise of apologetics a tangible proof for that which is intan-gible. With the strength and structure of this formal philosophical approach, Brewer's apologias offer explanation but more importantly contemplation. He adapts free verse to philosophical purposes. Epigraphs in many of the poems help him to sound more like a philosopher initiating a conversation with the reader.

Brewer's formal choice makes for a good one in allowing him to examine generational differences and to expose—without angst or condemna-tion—what lies behind family facades. "Apologia for Our Last Family Vaca-tion" explodes the myth that all family vacations are fun by juxtaposing the child's view ("We pick rotted, spiky fruit / and gag on it. Wipe chins with torn fingers. / Toss pulp to distract beaks from eyes, ears, privates") with the parents' view ("Mom and dad share a cigarette and stare out / from the deck of a flaming bungalow, time-share, / dream realized, ours for the next ten thousand years"). "Apologia for Missing Cousin Willie's Burial" depicts one family's pretense of sorrow at the funeral of an estranged relative who spent much of his time in jail and humiliated the kin: "Dad surprised at how many of the kids showed / even Berniece, crying, who hadn't / acknowledged her brother in years."

Certainly, Brewer does not avoid looking at his own profession of teaching in light of incongruities. In "Apologia for 'The Yolk of Marriage,'" the speaker bemoans the errors of student compositions with the compassion of one whose "fingers too are resistant and stiff, they too / at the mercy of years and some greater judgment." And in "Apologia for My Morning at the Milton Conference," the speaker refuses to ignore the incongruity of the responses to both the content and people at a conference presentation. Although "Current discussion details Augustine, et. al., / concoction of Satan, from Old Testament tidbits," the speaker confesses " ... I am distracted by the hatred I feel / for blonde hair, shaved nape, and herringbone shoulder / of the joker in front of me who leans further" and "To my left, a twitchy young guy spends the hour / reading his own essay, 'Conscience in *Lyddas*.'" Perhaps "Apologia for an Uninvited Disciple" qualifies as the most thought-provoking of the poems on teaching. "If he's one of mine, /" the speaker announces, "I need him dangerous when he paddles away / from this island in flames. The answer to the exam, / no one can teach—he is obliged to be happy."

Brewer's gift for sensory detail is most evident in his poems dealing with nature, such as "Apologia for a September Garden," "Apologia to the First Snake of the Year," "Apologia for Rain," and "Apologia for Morning Fog." "Apologia for the Indifference of Animals" points up the incongruity of human indifference and animal indifference, with human indifference always the more destructive, and nowhere in the book is the relationship between people and animals more poignant than in poems such as "Apologia for My Dog's Happiness, with a Motif of Chekhov" and "Apologia on the Eve of Jasper's 12th Birthday" which allude to dog and master, or perhaps person and master.

In the first poem of the book, "Apologia for a Modest Skull Collection," the speaker contemplates whether he has indeed invited his two sightseers into his library or they have instead interloped on his privacy, but he continues to show them his trophies nonetheless, meanwhile instructing them to look—"But not to touch." Paradoxically, throughout *Let me Explain*, Brewer welcomes his reader to look *and* to touch, to experience *and* to contemplate, and his invitation is well worth accepting.

New Madrid

Drunk in Sunlight
by Daniel Anderson
Johns Hopkins University Press, 2007
88 pages
$ 16.95

Reviewed by Jeremy Byars

Drunkenness in itself proves a significant theme in Daniel Anderson's second poetry collection *Drunk in Sunlight*. Exquisite natural and man-made details such as the "key-lime lather [that] spreads across / The pond," the porch lamp that "burns like a stroke of genius" and a "hundred parts of broken glass [that] / Begin their figuration into stones" intoxicate the reader with their lavishness. Images are lush, descriptions are graceful, and sorrow is omnipresent The reader is compelled to join in cherishing the momentary beauty of the world, obligated, as it were, to grow "absolutely drunk / On something. Something like belief."

One virtue of Anderson's poems is that they are highly accessible. The worlds of *Drunk in Sunlight* are familiar and uncomplicated. Readers are placed in such common landscapes as a field full of sunflowers in the aptly titled, "Sunflowers in a Field," a rural back road in the poem "Cycling," and a pond complete with cattails and dragonflies in "The Pond in Summertime." Beyond the "cold colors smoldering there" that "Seemed like the colors of despair / Or some unnamable regret" is the recognizable image of autumn in "Early Autumn in Tennessee." So too, the language of the poems is vernacular and not blanketed by a need to be grandiose. Even the most casual of read-ers can enter a poem like "In Minnesota Once," which begins, "Consider how the light rain falls, / How imperceptibly the water beads / A row of gems along the gutter's lip." `

My favorite poem is "Cycling." As it is in most if not all of Anderson's poems, the iambic meter here is tight and crisp, almost emulating the very move-ments of the cyclist-speaker: "I pumped. I cranked and pedaled past." Such phrases as "the bloodbeat thunder in your chest" and "the sudden whipcrack clarity of love"—the latter of which not only unexpectedly hits us with the weighty abstraction of love but also startles us with the spondee in the third measure—give dynamism to the rhythm. This poem, more than any other, exemplifies exactly how, in the process of living our daily lives, we can become drunk on belief.

While the poems tend to be harrowing and dark in their observation of our fallen, ever-changing world, they are often funny—wry even. Anderson's dry humor, emergent in his first book *January Rain*, returns here, and one cannot refrain from smiling or laughing even upon reading many of the poems. In "Thorns. Thistles.," the speaker catalogues how many Thanksgiving meals, Presidential elections, and shaves he's got left on earth according to an actuary. The poem is comedic even in the face of sorrow, as the speaker recognizes *"Two times a year, or so, / (Which roughly comes to seventy in all) / I'll cry myself to sleep."* In "America the Beautiful," the speaker gently satirizes candidates' responses to questions in a Miss America pageant.

One cannot stress enough the realization that the reader of *Drunk in Sunlight* is compelled to join Anderson in revering the momentary beauty of the world. As the speaker of "Aubade" remarks, "It never hurts to be reminded though, / How excellent it is to be alive."

Contributors' Notes

Margrethe Ahlschwede has published stories and essays in many journals including the *Seattle Review, South Dakota Review, Sou'wester,* and *Writing on the Edge.* She is professor of English at The University of Tennessee at Martin and also a quiltmaker and a grandmother.

Dianne Aprile has published four books, including two (*Place of Peace and Paradox and Making A Heart for God*) on the Abbey of Gethsemani, the monastery where the writer Thomas Merton lived. While a staff writer for *The Louisville Courier-Journal,* she shared a staff Pulitzer Prize and won the National Society of Newspaper Columnists' top award. She is currently on the faculty of the brief residency MFA in Writing program at Spalding University.

Brian Barker recently published his first book, *The Animal Gospels,* which won the Tupelo Press Editors' Prize. His poems, reviews, and interviews have appeared in such journals as *Poetry, Agni, Quarterly West, American Book Review, The Writer's Chronicle, The Indiana Review, Blackbird, Sou'wester,* and *River Styx.* He is Assistant Professor of English and Coordinator of Undergraduate Creative Writing at Murray State University.

E.A. Baxter III is the author of *Captain Hooter at Niagra,* a novel forthcoming from Michigan State University Press, and *Looking for Niagra, a book of poems* (Slipstream Press, 1993), in addition to many small press publications. He is the recipient of a NYS Caps Award for Fiction and a Just Buffalo Award. "Thought of the Week" is an excerpt from a creative nonfiction manuscript, *American Digression,* a work in progress.

Don Boes has published two books of poems: *Railroad Crossing and The Eighth Continent.* He is the recipient of three Al Smith Fellowships from the Kentucky Arts Council and has also been awarded residencies at The MacDowell Colony and Ragdale. He teaches in the Humanities Department at Bluegrass Community and Technical College.

Dixon Boyles has published fiction in *The Greensboro Review* and currently serves as the chair of Arts and Sciences at Beaufort County Community College in Washington, North Carolina, where he also teaches English.

Gaylord Brewer is a professor at Middle Tennessee State University, where he edits *Poems & Plays.* His most recent books of poetry are *Let Me Explain* (Iris Press, 2006) and, forthcoming, *The Martini Diet* (Dream Horse Press, 2007). His work also appears in *Best American Poetry 2006.*

Bill Brown is the author of two chapbooks, three poetry collections and a writing textbook. His new collection, *Tatters,* is forthcoming from March Street Press. The recipient of many writing fellowships and teaching awards, he lectures part-time at Peabody College of Vanderbilt University. He has new work in *Atlanta Review, Prairie Schooner,* and *The North American Review.*

Rick Campbell is the author of *The Traveler's Companion* (Black Bay Books, 2004) and *Setting The World In Order* (Texas Tech 2001). *Dixmont,* another collection, is forthcoming from Autumn House Press. His poems and essays have appeared in *The Georgia Review, The Missouri Review, Puerto Del Sol, Prairie Schooner,* and other journals. He is the director of Anhinga Press and the Anhinga Prize for Poetry, and he teaches English at Florida A&M University in Tallahassee, Florida. He lives with his wife and daughter in Gadsden County, Florida.

Richard Cecil is the author, most recently, of *Twenty First Century Blues,* a book of poems. He teaches at Indiana University, Bloomington.

Mick Cochrane is the author of two novels: *Flesh Wounds* (Nan Talese/Doubleday 1997, Penguin 1999), named a finalist in Barnes and Noble's Discover Great New Writers competition, and *Sport* (St. Martin's 2001, University of Minnesota Press 2002). He has published short stories in *Northwest Review, Kansas Quarterly, Cincinnati Review, Minnesota Monthly*, and *Water~Stone.* Currently he is professor of English and Lowry writer-in-residence at Canisius College in Buffalo, NY.

Peter Conners is an Editor at BOA Editions. His poetry collection *Of Whiskey and Winter* is forthcoming from White Pine Press (September 2007). His story collection, *Emily Ate the Wind,* is forthcoming from Marick Press (April, 2008). He edited *PP/FF: An Anthology* (Starcherone Books, 2006). He is founding co-editor of *Double Room.* Recent publications include *Poetry International, Mississippi Review, Verse, Fiction International, Salt Hill, Mid-American Review,* and *The Bitter Oleander.*

Silvia Curbelo is the author of three collections of poems, *Ambush, The Secret History of Water,* and *The Geography of Leaving.* Her poems have been published widely in literary journals and in more than two dozen anthologies, including *The Body Electric: America's Best Poetry, Snakebird: Thirty Years of Anhinga Poets,* and *Norton's Anthology of Latino Literature.* A native of Cuba, Curbelo lives in Tampa, Florida, and is managing editor for *Organica* magazine.

Brent Fisk is a writer from Bowling Green, Kentucky. His work appears in recent issues of *Rattle, Southern Poetry Review, and Southeast Review.* He has been nominated for three Pushcarts and recently received the Willow Review Award for his poem, "At the Babysitter's, Age Eight."

Malcolm Glass is a writer and photographer who has published five books of poems, including *Bone Love* and *The Dinky Line.* He and Bill Brown are the co-authors of Important Words, a textbook for writers of poetry. His plays have been produced in New York and by several universities and local theatres. He and his wife Mitzi team-teach writing workshops for area writers and high school students.

Fred Haefele is the author of the motorcycle memoir, *Rebuilding the Indian* (Riverhead Books, Bison Books, 2005). His essays have appeared in *Outside, Wired, The New York Times Magazine, American Heritage,* and other publications. He has received literary fellowships from The Fine Arts Work Center, the NEA, and Stanford University. He lives in Montana with his wife and two children and teaches in Murray State University's low-residency MFA program.

Jeff Hardin is the author of two chapbooks *(Deep in the Shallows and The Slow Hill Out)* as well as one collection, *Fall Sanctuary,* which won the Nicholas Roerich Prize. Recent and forthcoming publications include poems in *Ploughshares, Saint Ann's Review, Poem, Ascent, Nimrod, The Florida Review, Zone 3* and others. He teaches at Columbia State Community College in Columbia, TN.

Bill Hemminger teaches English and French at the University of Evansville. He has published poetry, essays, and short fiction, along with academic essays and translations. A recipient of three Fulbright awards, he has worked and taught in Madagascar, Cameroon, Senegal and El Salvador. He won a 1994 Syndicated Fiction Writers prize.

Holly Goddard Jones is the author of many short stories which have appeared or are forthcoming in *The Kenyon Review, The Southern Review, Epoch, The Gettysburg Review,* and elsewhere, and her work will be reprinted in *New Stories from the South: The Year's Best, 2007,* guest-edited by Edward P. Jones. "Good Girl," which originally appeared in *The Southern Review,* was honored with a "Special Mention" in *Pushcart Prize XXXI: Best of the Small Presses.* She is assistant professor in creative writing at Murray State University.

Janet McNally has published fiction in *The Iron Horse Literary Review* and *Traffic East.* She holds an MFA from Notre Dame.

James Scruton is the author, most recently, of *Galileo's House,* winner of the 2004 Poetry Prize from Finishing Line Press. He has poems forthcoming or in recent issues of *Poetry East, Louisville Review, Amoskeag,* and *New Delta Review.*

Charles Semones has published work in *The Chattahoochee Review, The Journal of Kentucky Studies, The Mennonite,* and *The South Carolina Review.* His collection, *Afternoon in the Country of Summer: New and Selected Poems* (Wind Publications, 2003) was awarded the Kentucky Literary Award for Poetry at the Southern Kentucky Book Fest in 2004.

Leah Stewart is the author of *Body of a Girl* (Viking/Penguin, 2000), which won the Mary Ruffin Poole Award for First Fiction and the Sir Walter Raleigh Award for best book by a North Carolina writer. Her second novel, *The Myth of You and Me* (Shaye Areheart Books, 2005), was chosen for both the September Book Sense list and Target's Breakout Books program. She was the 2006-2007 Nancy and Rayburn Watkins Visiting Professor of Creative Writing at Murray State University.

Thom Ward has published several poetry collections, including *Various Orbits* (Carnegie Mellon University Press, 2004) and *Small Boat with Oars of Different Size* (Carnegie Mellon, 2000) , as well a chapbook, *Tumblekid,* which won the 1998 Devil's Millhopper Poetry Contest. He is Editor for BOA Editions, Ltd. and lives with his wife and children in upstate New York.

Patricia Waters was born and reared in Nashville, Tennessee. She took her B.A. from Memphis State University, her M.A. and Ph.D. from the University of Tennessee Knoxville. Her first book of poems *The Ordinary Sublime* was published by Anhinga Press. She taught this year at the University of Alabama and she has her home in Athens, Tennessee.

Brian Weinberg has published fiction in *New Letters, Northwest Review, Bellevue Review, Meridian,* and *Notre Dame Review.* He has taught fiction writing at the University of Virginia, the University of Kentucky, and the Carnegie Center for Literacy and Learning, and served as the '04–'05 Writer-In-Residence at St. Albans School in Washington, DC.

Patti White teaches creative writing at the University of Alabama. She is the author of two collections of poems, *Tackle Box* (2002) and *Yellow Jackets* (2007), both published by Anhinga Press. The title poem of Tackle Box was made into an award-winning short film in 2003 (www.tackleboxthemovie.com). Her current project is a play about the apocalypse.

Acknowledgements

"Good Girl" by Holly Goddard Jones originally appeared in *The Southern Review,* Volume 41, Number 3, Summer 2005. Reprinted by permission of the author.

Reviewers

Jeremy Byars has published in such journals as *Gihon River Review, Ottawa Arts Review, Muscadine Lines* and *storySouth* and is currently finishing an annotated bibliography of the Towneley cycle plays.

Kevin Marshall Chopson teaches AP English Language and Composition, Poetry 101, and Creative Nonfiction at Davidson Academy in Nashville. His poetry has been published in the *English Journal, Cellar Roots,* and other small journals.

Daniel Dowell received a Bachelor's degree in Philosophy from Western Kentucky University and is currently on the Library Resources Staff at Madisonville Community College.

Gregory Hagan is a professor of English at Madisonville Community College. His work has been published in *The Journal of Kentucky Studies, Pudding, Another Chicago Magazine,* the now defunct *Redneck Review of Literature,* and other small magazines.

Chris Meredith recently graduated from the University of Tennessee, Knoxville. He lives in Illinois.

Vince Tweddell lives in Frankfort, where he writes for the *Frankfort State Journal.* A short story of his won third place in the *2006 Louisville Eccentric Observer's* fiction contest.

Morgan Williams works as a freelance writer. His poem "Icarus" was published in the summer 2006 edition of *The Blind Man's Rainbow.*

Jenna Wright, a faculty member at the University of Tennessee at Martin and co-director of the writing center, teaches fiction writing, advanced grammar, and British literature. Her writing has been published in *Poetry Analysis: Understanding and Critiquing Poetry, The Tennessee English Journal, The Tennessee Writer, The Delta Kappa Gamma Bulletin,* and other journals.

Sarah Gutwirth – Artist's Statement

I am interested in the decorative arts and the design of interior spaces and how they derive much of their imagery from forms in nature that are reiterated and re-articulated. My current work includes human-made objects of a decorative nature. I am interested in what a painting seeks to make present and how those aspects are in dialogue with its architectural and decorative setting. I think of my paintings as intended for domestic spaces: reflective of the kinds of collecting and decorating activities that humans use to adorn those spaces,.

I grew up visiting period rooms in museums, and have had the opportunity to travel quite widely to see artworks in their intended spaces as well as in many museums. I retain intensely the sense of how a painting functions in a space of worship or a living space, integrated with architecture and décor, and subject to the light of windows as well as to other sources of light. I am thinking more consciously about the articulation of space in a painting, relating this to the objects and places we humans inhabit, but also to the illusionistic and contradictory spaces of paintings. Among other things, these works explore painted spaces, which serve as the frames or precincts for other virtual paintings (within the painting). This is not about art history as a distanced academic subject, however, but more as an extension of the language of decorative/imaginative environments as they were meant to be incorporated into lived spaces.

Sarah Gutwirth received her BFA and BA degrees in 1978 from a joint program of Reed College and the Pacific Northwest College of Art. Her MFA is from Pratt Institute in New York City. She has had 14 one and two person exhibits over the last twenty-four years and has had work in numerous group shows as well. Her work is in several collections, and she has received grants from Kentucky Arts Council, Kentucky Foundation for Women, Murray State University and United University Professions at SUNY. After holding positions in painting at Georgia Southern University and SUNY Potsdam, she is currently Associate Professor of Painting at Murray State University in Murray, Kentucky.

Sarah Gutwirth, *Kabinet 2006*, oil on canvas, 22 x 22",
Collection of Yvonne Bless.

New Madrid